W9-ABH-637

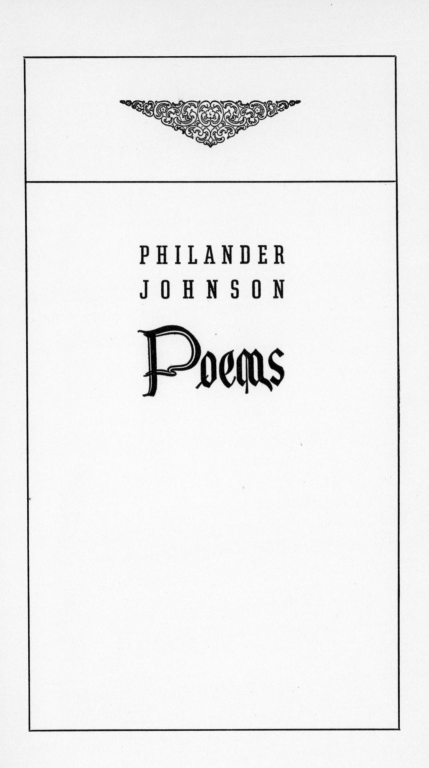

PHILANDER
JOHNSON

Poems

PHILANDER JOHNSON

POEMS

A selection of his poems that appeared in the Washington Evening Star with additional poems from his writings.

RUFUS H. DARBY PRINTING CO.

WASHINGTON, DC

CARL A. RUDISILL
LIBRARY
LENOIR RHYNE COLLEGE

811
g63p

COPYRIGHT 1942 BY
MARY ADAMS JOHNSON

24539
Sept 48

To the Washington Evening Star, considerate friend of many years, and to the newspapers and magazines that complimented the author and brightened the long road by copying his poems and paragraphs from the column "Shooting Stars," this book of verse is dedicated.

M. A. J.

Philander Johnson

Foreword

Philander Johnson was a native of Wheeling, W. Va., born February 6, 1866. His parents were Sylvanus E. and Martha A. Mann Johnson, and he grew to maturity in a home distinguished for its cultural atmosphere. Formal educational opportunities were his for the asking, but he was largely self-taught and took honorable pride in the fact. Particularly, from the beginning of his professional career, he was interested in newspapers—as educational media in the best meaning of the term.

Much of his boyhood Mr. Johnson spent in Cincinnati, Ohio, where his father was a member of the staff of the Enquirer. Subsequently, while still a youth, he followed his parents to Washington—an "accident" resulting from the senior Mr. Johnson's assignment to represent his paper in the Nation's Capital.

But the lad was not altogether dependent upon his father for the bent of his mind or for his first success. Equipped with talents notably his own, he began to write almost as soon as he had learned to read. His apprentice efforts were published in the Merchant Traveler, Chicago, and led to his employment as a contributor to many other publications. A natural enthusiasm for the theater resulted in his appointment as dramatic critic on the old Sunday Capital Weekly. Later, he held similar positions on the Washington Post and the Washington Evening Critic.

Joining the staff of the Washington Evening Star, July 15, 1891, Mr. Johnson's service between that date and the close of his life included the writing of many thousands of editorial paragraphs and, especially, the material carried daily on the editorial page under the heading "Shooting Stars". Also, for a period he was dramatic editor and an occasional contributor of news and feature stories of miscellaneous character.

Mr. Johnson still was a young man when he attained the heights of his chosen field of journalism. Thereafter during more than four decades he enjoyed an international reputation for his pithy, humorous comments on "the passing show". He was quoted systematically in the press of Europe as well as in that of America.

Scores of common epigrams repeated by literally millions of people were of his invention. He is credited with having sponsored "Cheer up, the worst is yet to come", "Don't throw a monkey wrench into the machinery" and many other popular sayings.

Many of the "personalities" of Mr. Johnson's column were represented at a party tendered him in 1922 in recognition of the 31st anniversary of his engagement as a Star writer. "Senator Sorghum", "Farmer Corntassel", "Uncle Eben", "Cactus Joe of Crimson Gulch" and others were among the figures portrayed by their creator's friends.

Inevitably, much of his production was reprinted in book form. "Too good to lose," his quaintly satirical political observations passed into permanent literature in volumes entitled "Sayings of Uncle Eben" and "Senator Sorghum's Primer of Politics". He also brought out a collection of selected verse, "Now-a-Day Poems". His ballad, "Somewhere in France Is the Lily", set to music, was sung on the battlefront during the First World War.

Presidents, members of Congress, the governors of States and many eminent men and women who never sought public office but were content to contribute to the welfare of their country in private fashion commended him for his wisdom, his gracefulness of expression, his sensitive humanitarian point of view. It was remarked of him as evidence of his instinctive modesty that he never allowed the first person singular pronoun to enter his column.

Mr. Johnson was a member of the Gridiron Club and wrote for its famous dinners some political sketches which still are remembered. He also was affiliated with the National Press Club and the Association of Oldest Inhabitants of the District of Columbia. It should be mentioned likewise that he was a 32d degree Mason, a member of King Solomon, No. 31, Blue Lodge, and of Almas Temple.

His interest in music brought him keen and lasting pleasure, he was enthusiastic about artistic effort of every sort, was fond of traveling, loved the sea, delighted in the companionship of children. In religion, he was a Swedenborgian. His Americanism was traditional. He was the great, great grandson of Peter Johnson, who came from Holland to Pennsylvania in the 18th century and the great grandson of a lieutenant in the militia in the Revolution and the grandson of a private in the War of 1812.

The final years of Mr. Johnson's life were spent in congenial comfort at his home *"Dawnwood"* on the Rockville Pike, near Rockville, Md. He died at George Washington University Hospital, Washington, May 18, 1939, and was buried in Rock Creek Cemetery.

News of his passing brought tributes to his memory from many unknown admirers throughout the United States. The Star paid editorial homage to him as follows:

"Philander Johnson was a survivor of the old school of American humorists which included Mark Twain, Eugene Field and James Whitcomb Riley. The professional wits and bards of today are of a different genus.

"Intelligence, keen yet not unkind, and imagination were Mr. Johnson's natural qualifications. Yet they were not his only endowment. He was a philosopher and a wit in his daily verse and on special occasions gave evidence of the inspiration of the true poet. He also was an excellent craftsman in letters; his work was disciplined and controlled by his sympathies and by a certain compelling anxiety for perfection. Each line of his manuscript was scrupulously neat because he wished it so to be. His penmanship was that of an artist who loves chirography for its own sake. Trained as a reporter, he remained always a devotee of accuracy. His search throughout his whole career was for the right word for the right thought.

"Of course, he was intimately acquainted with life, a prodigious reader of the news of the world, a skilled observer of human wisdom and human folly. Literary expression, to him, was as normal an exercise as seeing or hearing. He was far less 'a fellow of infinite jest' than a philosophic commentator on all that was whimsical in the passing scene. His pen was sharp, but—let it be repeated

—not uncharitable. The masks he invented for his teaching . . . were a congenial company; his readers developed an affection for them as well as for their sponsor.

"Any appraisal of his achievement must take into account the fact that Mr. Johnson was distinctively an American, proud and happy to be a product of a democratic civilization and eager to serve its noblest purposes. Even when the skies were darkened, he kept his faith unspoiled, retained his optimism undiminished."

Theodore W. Noyes

L'Envoi

It seems ages since Philander Johnson put down his pen for the last time in the Spring of 1939. Great events of a tragic significance have occurred. The world is engaged in a colossal struggle in which two groups of nations contest for dominion over human destiny. What next may happen to civilization is beyond the power of the average person to guess. Cataclysmic change prevails, and the end is far.

But the species cannot be fated to perish from the tortured earth. To believe the race doomed to extinction —or to slavery—would be to question the integrity of the Architect of the Universe.

Four qualities in the soul of the individual prompt confident belief in the survival of human society. Wisdom, humor, fellowship, hopefulness: all these are assets in such a season of trial and tribulation. Generously endowed with them, plain and humble men and women will not despair.

No more appropriate occasion, then, could be chosen for the publication of a book of Philander Johnson's writings. He was possessed of the essential American capacity to learn by experience, to laugh at trouble, to be charitable and optimistic. His country needs his contribution now as perhaps never before. And it would give him delight to be of such use in the current crisis.

Index

AN IDEAL

Each to his fancy.   Some there be who love the radiance
    rare
Of soft light as it lingers o'er a ball-room favorite's hair,
The silken murmurings that sound where beauty lightly
    glides,
And some there be who love to cross the world with
    martial strides.
But compliments are sorry dross; a smile is oft a mask,
And life's a long, hard journey where deceit's too much to
    ask.
So give me, now and then, a nook along the weary pike,
With time enough to sit and talk with fellows that I like.

THE MAN AND THE JOB

"They told me that I ought to score
Five days of work each week; no more.
And on these days I ought to fix
My hours at eight, or even six.
For many an hour I'll feel alone,
Away from friends I long have known.
I say, as memory brings a sigh,
We've been good pals, my job and I.

"In time of weariness and care
Here was the friend who helped me bear
Suspense and disappointment grim
And whispered as the light grew dim;
Another day of joy you'll see
If you will just stay close to me.
Beneath a bright or shadowy sky
We've been good pals, my job and I.

"Perhaps we've quarreled now and then
A little—and made up again.
When we would meet from day to day
You made the time with hope seem gay.
The thought you'd bring was one of cheer,
Though oft your teaching seemed severe.
To stick together let us try;
We've been good pals—my job and I."

OUTDOOR PREFERENCE

The grave astronomers have told
    Some facts of deepest meaning.
Yet I for calculations bold
    Have very little leaning.
Our nomad ancestors afar
    Had taste. I cannot flout it.
I'd rather gaze upon a star
    Than read a book about it.

THE LAND OF YESTERDAY

When the time of toil is ended and the stars begin to show,
And the firelight fades and flickers and the shadows come
 and go;
When the present day is fading through the portals of the
 past
To join the other days that made the journey all too fast,
You can't help going with it far enough to say "good-by,"
And maybe it will take your hand and lead you; and you
 try
To laugh and hope, just as you did when everything was
 new
And you were living in the land of things you meant to
 do.

It takes you to the rainbow which showed treasure's hiding
 place;
It shows youth's starting point, where all were equal in
 the race.
The winter's fierceness there was all forgotten in a day,
For nothing was so real as the blossoming of May.
The stars that shine afar then seemed so radiantly near
That one might pluck them from the sky, should he but
 persevere.
Life's fairest, truest joys are those too fair to e'er be true,
They dwell back yonder in the land of things we meant
 to do.

THE UNIVERSAL POEM

He who is thrilled when blossoms rise
To borrow beauty from the skies,
Or finds a pleasure in the glow
Of sunlight on the silvered snow,
Or pauses a great hymn to hear
When winds are sounding fiercely near,
Like each of us, of life a part—
He has a poem in his heart.

[3]

AN OLD STORY

"I haven't any chance," he said, "the world has closed
    the door
Of opportunity that opened to the men of yore.
The songs have all been sung. The mighty tasks are
    carried through.
The world no longer young, leaves nothing more for youth
    to do."

He watched the steamship hasten on its journey far away
To the lands that oped their treasures to us only
    yesterday.
He saw the locomotive as it labored hard for speed,
Its efforts insufficient for a waiting public's need.

He heard the voices calling from the wilderness so deep
"Come ye, with hearts of courage; come and waken from
    their sleep.
The harvests that for centuries have waited 'neath our
    soil,
Impatient for the cheery call of common sense and toil."

The air is all a-whisper with the messages that fly
To tell of years more wondrous than the wondrous years
    gone by.
And still he cries, "I have no chance!" and still the world
    sweeps on,
Nor heeds the plaint that it has heard since ages past and
    gone.

REFINEMENT OF KIDNAPING

Gossip, with an insidious word
In cruel purpose may be heard,
    As with determination
She undertakes a sad surprise
And, in an innocent disguise,
    Kidnaps a reputation.

TO A SCHOOL OF JOURNALISM

A man whose hair was thin and white
    And yet whose eyes flashed fire
Remarked, "Excuse me while I smite
    A reminiscent lyre.
The poetry which now we see
    In superabundant yield
Don't measure up, it seems to me,
    To two lines of 'Gene Field.
The heavy economic guff,
    Which now they bravely quote,
Seems but a bluff compared to stuff
    That Horace Greely wrote.
The satire that they now employ
    Seems faint and insincere.
You should have had a taste my boy
    Of Charles A. Dana's sneer.
'Tis true we're getting all the news,
    Yet these men stand alone.
Though other men may fill their shoes,
    Their pens are still their own.
So, hit your old typewriter, son,
    And pifflicate and spout.
Let the devouring presses run
    Till the wood pulp gives out.
I don't believe you'll hit the pace—
    Although I hope you may—
The eloquence and simple grace
    Of that departed day
When men sought honor and applause
    And scorned their pay to scan—
When men wrote what they felt, because
    They loved their fellow man."

A SIMPLE SERMON

There's only one method of meetin' life's test;
Jes' keep on a-strivin' an' hope fur the best.
Don't give up the game an' retire in dismay
'Cause hammers are thrown when you'd like a bouquet.

This world would be tiresome, we'd all get blues
If all the folks in it held the same views;
So finish your work; show the best of your skill,
Some people won't like it, but other folks will.

If you're leadin' an army, or buildin' a fence,
Do the most that you kin with your own common sense.
One small word of praise in this journey of tears
Outweighs in the balance 'gainst cart loads of sneers.

The plants that we're passin' as commonplace weeds
Oft prove to be jes' what some sufferer needs.
So keep on a-goin'; don't stay standin' still—
Some people won't like you, but other folks will.

THE BENEFICIARIES

Some grain, placed yonder in the snow,
Attracts the starling or the crow,
The sparrow and the flaunting jay,
The mocking bird with stifled lay,
The red bird with resplendent crest—
Each comes in eager selfish quest,
With rivalry that gives no heed
To one another's urgent need.
Their own existence thus pursued
Is their sufficient gratitude.
As by the window there we stand
With new supply for more demand
They look on us as creatures sent
By nature, for their comfort meant,
And as each stranger comes and goes,
We say, "Perhaps we are—who knows?"

[6]

A TOAST

Oh, here's to the fool with the bauble and bells!
The song that he sings and the story he tells
Assume to be neither persuasive nor wise,
But only the trifles that wit may devise.
He asks your approval, but never your trust,
While he babbles along as he may or he must.

He does not appear in the garb of the sage,
As a vender of wisdom for youth and for age,
Nor pose as a strictly self-qualified saint
To indulge his own greed while he counsels restraint.
Though his jest and his song we but scantily prize,
Here's a toast to the fool who assumes no disguise!

THE OTHER MAN

When fortune crowns some enterprise
    Behold the crowd that gathers near
To claim the credit and seem wise.
    How mightily they persevere,
While modest worth is thrust aside!
    Their lusty chorus rends the sky
As each cries out in stubborn pride:
    "Behold your hero!   It was I!"

But when misfortune grimly waits
    Where glory seemed at first to smile,
Deserted are the temple gates
    Where fame was worshipped for a while.
Now doubt and mystery are spread
    Though once so simple seemed the plan,
For each when questioned shakes his head
    And says, "It was the other man."

[7]

TWO VOLUMES

Two volumes standing side by side
Tell of a lifetime's toil and pride.
One is a tome full stoutly built
And brave with decorative gilt.
Its pages numerous are all
Close-covered with a fluent scrawl
Save where, as Fancy sped along,
She left a picture or a song.

The other is a flimsy tract
With lettering painfully exact.
The work of plodding, patient years
Writ out in ink oft thinned with tears.
The first holds what I thought I knew
In years gone by. And volume Two,
With blots, and pages torn away,
Is what I'm sure I know today.

LONG AGO

The lights on every hand shone fair,
    Full sprightly was the passing jest;
And laughter rippled through the air
    And echoed with increasing zest.
The hours sped gladly on their way
    Like sun-lit waters as they flow—
But all this happened yesterday,
    And yesterday is long ago.

The ice that tinkled in the glass
    Now presses 'gainst an aching brow,
To still its pulsing—'tis, alas,
    The difference 'twixt then and now!
There was a time when all were gay
    With every joy life could bestow;
That was a time called yesterday—
    But yesterday is long ago.

THOSE ABSENT

You men who have deserved the deepest joy;
  You men who bravely fought and nobly fell,
You may not join the throng where we employ
  What means we have our gratitude to tell.
Afar you rest, where freemen lift the cheer,
  Nor claim the tribute even of a tear.

You men who fell that little babes might turn
  With trustful smiling to their mother's eyes;
You who have passed the shadowy way to learn
  The lessons which this mortal world denies,
We cannot doubt, amid the grand accord,
  The love we bear you must be some reward.

SUBMERGED

The little things that fretted us—
  How trifling they appear—
The overcrowded omnibus!
  The rainy day so drear!
The sneer that thoughtless envy flings!
  The luckless games we play!
We have a lot of other things
  To think about today.

How we disdain the trifling ills
  That hurt us in the past
When once the call of Duty thrills
  Across the country vast.
The small success—the vain regret—
  'Tis like an idle dream.
The things which used to make us fret—
  How frivolous now they seem!

[9]

SUBJECTIVE

To the miser the moon is a coin of bright gold;
  To the warrior a bullet it seems;
To the lover, a lantern which Cupid may hold
  To light up the pathway of dreams.

To the sage 'tis a strangely mysterious realm,
  Whose study his life might employ;
To the sailor a guide as he stands at the helm;
  To the infant a coveted toy.

And the face that it frames every night smiles anew
  At the loves and the hatreds we find;
Since impressions depend on a man's point of view
  And likewise the state of his mind.

GONE BUT NOT FORGOTTEN

A resolution once I made
  With stanch and solemn show;
Its purport carefully I weighed
  Some few short weeks ago.

But change doth rapidly befall,
  And with a furrowing brow
I vainly struggle to recall
  That resolution now.

'Tis like the rose that bloomed so fair
  And vanished 'neath the frost;
'Tis like the cloud that rode the air
  Awhile, and then was lost.

Unto the darkness of my woe
  One gleam of comfort clings,
My resolutions fade, but so
  Do other beauteous things.

MOTHER

I've heard the music that takes wings
From pipe and horn and trembling strings.
I've marveled at the glorious art
Whose mystery thrills the human heart.
But I endeavor all in vain
To recollect some splendid strain.
Instead comes echoing sweet and low
A simple song of long ago.
'Tis but a dear old-fashioned hymn.
With memory mists my eyes grow dim,
And as I listen there appears
A face with tenderest smiles or tears.
It is no song by genius wrought,
All cunningly devised and taught.
A mother-song, it soothes my ear
With love unselfish and sincere.
I've read some poets who amaze
With splendid thought and dazzling phrase;
I've read philosophers and feared
Their wisdom as they subtly sneered.
Such words, though wondrous they may be,
Have small significance to me
Compared to that old hymn so sweet
That told of mother-love complete.

JUNE

O June, sweet June, so well beloved and fair,
  Since you are gone the sky is overcast,
And there is sadness in the autumn air
  That sighs and softly whispers of the past.

A gentle memory is all that's left,
  And where the dew has dropt its farewell tear,
The rose, all melancholy and bereft,
  Flings its last fragrant petal on the bier.

LIFE

How strange is this human existence!
   'Tis burdened with terrible doubt.
Though we study with honest persistence,
   It's a problem that no one makes out.

If environment's wholly propitious
   And heredity gives a good start,
Perhaps you'll get some of the wishes
   You've cherished so near to your heart.

Men's methods or pull or position
   Make distinctions not easy to see.
What for A would mean instant perdition
   Is excusable business for B.

Life's a great hypothetical query
   That often seems prosy and long.
No wonder some of us get weary
   And find we have answered it wrong.

SELF-AFFLICTION

Men do today as men have ever done,
   Asking for leadership that will evade
The rough and weary course that must be run,
   With mysteries that will leave us oft afraid.

Men ask for promises and still forgive
   If promises that seemed at first so fair
Are unfulfilled and we are left to live
   Under the burden of still greater care.

We lift our arms and with a gesture wide
   Before the world in satisfaction tell
Of all our confidence and all our pride
   Since we ourselves have forged our fetters well.

CHAINED

I pray for wisdom and I crave
  The sweet content which goodness gives;
Yet rather would I be a slave,
  Who, fiercely pressed, 'midst striving lives,
Than he whom knowledge sets apart
  From human fellowship, to dwell
With plodding brain and shriveling heart,
  A prisoner in a book-bound cell.

And better the repentant tear
  That seeks to right some thoughtless wrong
Than cold perfection grown austere
  And distant from the struggling throng.
I shall not ask by hasty flight
  To shun all error and distress,
And dwell upon the mountain height
  And view the stars in loneliness.

FATE

Each rose that blooms ere long must fade;
  The sweetest song will be forgot;
The sunlight must give 'way to shade;
  Things are, one day; and next are not.
And yet the flower blossoms fine,
  Although its fate is surely writ.
Nor does the sun forbear to shine
Because the owl, ere long, must flit.
And little you and lesser I—
  Shall we behold the future vast
And breathe an apprehensive sigh
  For joys hard-won, that may not last?
Rejoice and cheer your fellow man,
  Nor grieve because time's knell must ring!
Be brave and happy as you can
  Till fate hands you the ding-a-ling.

A REFUGE

There's a still, cozy nook with a novel or two,
   And a generous armchair that beckons to rest,
And a jar of tobacco, whose wealth I may strew
   In and over the bowl of the pipe I like best.
And there, where the incense of indolence burns
   Above the big armchair, the pipe and the book,
It seems that life's labors, its devious turns,
   But lead, after all, to this still, cozy nook.

The noise of the world babbles distant and soft,
   And the cannon's dull rattle, the trumpets rude blare,
Would mellow, should War hurl his banner aloft,
   For gentleness only can penetrate there.
'Tis a spot that was ever a stranger to fear;
   A shelter 'gainst fate which no storm ever shook,
And the hours are my comrades, who whisper of cheer,
   With the generous armchair, the pipe and the book.

THE RIPPLE

Just a little splash—that's all
When you let a pebble fall
In the lake. The waters close
And in dignified repose
Picture back the hills and sun
Just as they have always done.
Everything seems as before;
Just a splash; and nothing more.

Mighty men and small ones, too,
Put on high, by fate, we view.
Shadows of forgetfulness
Soon surround them more or less.
Like the glistening waves they fade,
Those slight ripples that they made.
Recollection can recall
Just a little splash—that's all.

DISTRUST

I shall not say
   That she is fair.
I shall not trust
   My doting eyes.
I do no more
   Than to declare
That in her glance
   Is paradise.
For does she not
   In me discern
A man of grace
   And lofty mien,
To whom old Jove
   Himself might turn
For study of
   A pose serene?

Now, well I know
   That I am naught
Except a light
   And careless knave,
With narrow brow
   And legs ill wrought
And only fit
   To be her slave.
And if she sees
   Adonis there,
What conjuring may
   Mine own eyes do?
I shall not vow
   That she is fair,
I only say
   I love her true.

THE ROAD TO LAZYVILLE

Show me the road to Lazyville—
　It can't be far away—
Where shadows linger cool and still
　And idle sunbeams play.
Where rustling leaves are whispering soft,
　And skies are mild and blue,
And placid cloud-banks drift aloft,
　With nothing else to do.

Oh, Lazyville's a dear old place;
　It's over dreamland way;
The route's not difficult to trace
　Upon a summer day.
The nodding rose that blooms in state,
　The wild flowers on the hill,
All generously indicate,
　The way to Lazyville.

THE SONG SURVIVES

The shriek of mad machinery resounds
　Upon the sun-baked scene,
An airplane grumbles on its sullen rounds—
　And in between
　　I heard
　　A mocking bird!

A shot rings out and terror fills each heart
　And hatred's shaft is keen.
A simple song defies our angry art,
　For in between
　　I heard
　　A mocking bird.

TOO LATE!

When there's gayety assembled and the lights are all aglow,
Why is it that we falter in the conversation's flow?
Why is it that we do not think till half-past two or three
Of something which at ten would have been first-rate
     repartee?
  Repose declines to greet you. It is banished from your
     bed
  As you keep on thinking over all the things you might
     have said.

When your name has just been mentioned in connection
     with a speech,
And every thought you ever had has drifted out of reach,
When you say, "To public speaking, unaccustomed as I
     am,"
And then relapse into an imitation of a clam,
  You realize with bitterness that when three hours have
     fled
  You'll have insomnia, thinking of the things you might
     have said.

'Tis the fate of many a statesman with a crisis on his
     hands;
It's the same way with a lover who in bashful silence
     stands.
In every line of effort we are likely to be caught
In fierce resentment of some bright but useless after-
     thought.
  Of all the gloomy specters that oppress our souls with
     dread,
  The worst are recollections of the things we might have
     said.

OPULENCE

A sparrow on the window sill,
  In jaunty pride came balancing.
He flourished gaily, in his bill
  A shred of common wrapping string.
And all his manner plainly said.
  "What wonderful success is mine!
Let each in envy bow his head
  For I have found a bit of twine!

"Now luxury shall join with taste
  To furnish me a proper nest.
I have enough and some to waste
  Of what all birds esteem the best.
It is my very own by right,
  My treasure I shall not resign
Without a stern, relentless fight,
  For I have found this bit of twine."

Oh, man of empire, man of power,
  With treasure coveted by all,
Give welcome in this springtime hour
  Unto your comrade stanch, though small.
Let's spread the news; a mine has paid;
  A railway holds a rival line;
A fortune has been gained in trade;
  A sparrow's found a bit of twine.

OVERESTIMATION

If I as smart could only be
  As Mother Love once thought,
How easily I would set free
  A world in error caught.
But I must own in sad surprise,
  As disappointment wakes,
Even a Mother fond and wise
  May sometimes make mistakes.

THE ROAD
(U. S. Route 240)

I know a Road, a Winding Road;
Here a human stream has flowed
Through joys and sorrows, hopes and fears,
On current swift through many years.
Youth in its buoyancy we see
In hurrying quest of thoughtless glee
That pauses not before the shrine
Where patriots would their heads incline
In silent, reverent prayers for aid,
As an adventure bold was made
Far from the haunts of pleasure light
In quest of Liberty and Right.

Here rides the commerce from afar
On truck so stout, or graceful car;
Here in its traffic you will find
The treasure vast, or guiding mind;
And where the humble inn would care
For man and beast with honest fare.
Lights shine like stars midst colors gay
And bid men for assistance stay
That they securely may pursue
Their rapid courses till they view
The city that in Splendor gleams,
In bright fulfillment of the dreams
That for our brave forefathers glowed
And led them through the Winding Road.

Among the figures, one most fair
Again seems proudly riding there,
Seeking the duty to be done,
The Glorious Youthful Washington
Who followed in the gallant train
That stood with Braddock at Duquesne.

Here with uncovered head I stand
As mighty memories take command
Of blessings on mankind bestowed
By heroes of the Winding Road.

PRETENSION

He shunned the smile which, like the sunny gleam
　　That sparkles even on the deepest sea,
Strives o'er each human countenance to beam.
　　Stern was his judgment; final his decree.

He scorned the tears, this man of mental might,
　　Which, like the passing rains that softly flow
Upon the steadfast mountain's loftiest height,
　　Come 'mid the shadows that each heart must know.

Aloof he stood where simple friends were few.
　　Men journeyed far and at his feet would sit
To learn.　Yet deep within himself he knew
　　That they were wise and he a hypocrite.

ANTICIPATED

When you essay a gentle quip,
　　Some friend is sure to greet you with
The hint that you have made a slip,
　　"That joke was told by Sidney Smith."

Or if some comment you address
　　To human nature's curious ways,
A voice is sure to murmur, "Yes,
　　That's just what Dr. Johnson says."

Or if your soul is softly swept
　　By sentimental fancies sad,
'Tis just what Byron wrote, except
　　Your way of putting it is bad.

Of all the griefs that come your way
　　These sad reminders are the worst.
It makes no difference what you say,
　　Some other fellow said it first.

TRIUMPH

What is success? To hear above the din
    Of ruthless battle the barbarian's cry
For mercy; to exhort or boldly win
    The treasure that allures the envious eye;
To stand forth iron-nerved and pitiless
And rise o'er those who falter in the stress—
Is this success?

Or is it to reach forth and stoutly grasp
    The hand of him who weakens on the way,
And lead him on with firm and friendly clasp
    Toward high ideals—toward the light of day;
To speak the word of strength and kindliness,
To leave an honored name that men shall bless,
This is success!

THE DAY

A few brief hours of waking; that is all.
A few brief hours, and then the shadows fall
    And quell the tumult and the glaring light.
A golden dream of morning, mounting high;
A twilight purple in the Western sky.
    Only a little while and then, good night.

A wish is verified. Perhaps a fear
In stern reality's dread shape draws near.
    You've labored wrong—perchance you've toiled aright.
It matters not when all is dark and done
If you be he who lost or he who won.
    'Tis but a little while, and then, good night.

And hope shall whisper sweet and pride relent
As o'er the world the hastening hours are sent
    That men may measure striving by their flight.
The tiny present with its joy or pain
Shall fade. And day shall fade and shine again.
    'Tis but a little while and then, good night.

INCORRIGIBLE

It's kinder awful when I think
    Of hours I've fooled away,
A-lingerin' on the river's brink
    To watch the ripples play;
A-watchin' silvery clouds that float
    Acrost the crystal skies,
Or stoppin' by the hour to note
    The dancin' butterflies!

I might have been a-savin' coin
    An' pilin' bricks on stone,
An' findin' easy folks to join
    Their money with my own.
An' yet whene'er I think of it,
    My heart grows warm and gay,
I somehow don't begrudge a bit
    The hours I've fooled away!

STAR SPANGLED BANNER

"The Star Spangled Banner—oh, long may it wave
O'er the land of the free and the Home of the Brave!"
The words swiftly flow and the melody brings
A hope to the humble—a warning to kings.

The Star Spangled Banner—a hint from the sky
Of the majesty shown when our colors pass by.
And the words will ring true with the music so sweet
As with eager attention we rise to our feet.

CONCEALMENT

Each one of us has dropped a tear
    In secret now and then
For things that never will appear
    Unto our fellow men.
The road you travel may seem rough
    And hope be far away,
But still you throw a merry bluff
    And struggle to be gay.
For well you know that if you claim
    Of sympathy a share,
You're due to quit the busy game
    And sink into despair.
None but the thoughtless will reveal
    Life's bitterness and guile.
The wise endeavor to conceal
    The hurt beneath the smile.
So let us join to seek anew
    The passing thought that cheers,
The rainbow gently gleaming through
    The mist of human tears.
Let's boldly lift the song again
    In light and careless tone.
Our joys are for our fellow men;
    Our sorrows are our own.

REMEMBRANCE BLOOMS

I brought no blossoms for the friend so dear
    Who bade good-by and journeyed on his way.
The blossoms struggle in my garden here
    And bravely strive to smile from day to day.

I did not leave their withering loveliness
    A token of my grieving, deep and true;
I tend them still with memory's fond caress—
    I think, dear friend, 'tis as you'd have me do.

TRYING TO BE GOOD

When you were just a little boy
  "A-tryin' to be good,"
How frequently you would annoy
  The peaceful neighborhood
And hear your father say anew,
  As tears fell fast and hot,
"It hurts me, son, much more than you"—
  You knew that it did not.

Your brother laughed at your disgrace
  As you refused a chair,
Your mother kissed your tear-stained face
  And smiled and said, "There! There!"
For mothers more than all the rest
  Have always understood
How boys may fail who do their best
  "A-tryin' to be good."

It needs experience so stern
  To make life's pathway plain;
It needs a lot of years to learn
  To curb a restless brain.
Some boys grow up as men of note
  For courage, strength and skill,
And some, though old enough to vote,
  Don't learn, and never will.

If you should help at duty's call
  To mold the social plan,
Reproving follies great and small
  That fret your fellow man,
A moment now and then employ—
  T'would help you if you could—
With recollections of that boy
  "A-tryin' to be good."

A LETTER TO SANTA CLAUS

Dear Santa Claus: Assuming that you really exist,
Would you kindly put a grown-up, just for once, upon
  your list?
Nor hold it in resentment if he's sometimes been inclined
To question your existence, for a man may change his
  mind.
I've read of mental science and of telepathic waves,
And other things that show how strangely nature oft be-
  haves.
I've followed some great student far aloft beyond the
  stars,
'Til I really feel acquainted with the people up on Mars.
My skeptic mood has vanished, as for solemn thoughts I
  pause—
If all these things be true, why then, why not a Santa
  Claus?
I dimly recollect it was the custom long ago
To take a pen as Christmas day drew near to let you know
Exactly what would please your correspondent, so that you
Need not be worried guessing as to what 'twere best to do.
I shall not ask for sweets or toys to rob the children's store,
But, oh, I'd like to have my old-time appetite once more.
And I'd like to have some sunshine of the kind that used
  to gleam
Thro' my window when the waking was far sweeter than
  the dream.
I'd like to have some song birds, with melodies so sweet
That they seemed to set the wind-swept daisies dancing at
  my feet.
And I'd like to have my hope and faith and smiling as of
  old—
Please give me back my rainbow that shone o'er a pot of
  gold.
I beg, sir, to assure you that I shall appreciate
Your kindly offices, and hope I may reciprocate.
I thank you in advance for such attention as you may
Bestow on the above request
      Yours truly,   Olden Gray.

MIDAS

King Midas, in the days of old,
Turned everything he touched to Gold,
And, where vast splendors were on view,
The pangs of sad starvation knew.

King Midas now, reincarnate,
In gilded and superfluous state
Seeks for some thought of simple cheer
And hears the trembling voice of Fear.
He asks a song all freely sung
And hears the lisp of Flattery's tongue.
He turns unto Affection's quest
And only meets Self-interest.
He strives to cast his gold away
And it returns two-fold next day.

He craves some word of friendly cheer
And finds the smile that hides a sneer.

King Midas, midst his mighty store,
Still hungers as he did of yore.

THE DESTINATION

The earth, the water and the sky
Are ours; we delve or ride or fly,
And swifter still the pace we make,
Nor study well the course we take;
And yonder in the twilight gleams
A castle in the land of dreams.

Each as he journeys hopes to find
The spot where cares are left behind,
And hurries faster day by day,
Until his strength fails by the way—
And still before the nightfall gleams
The splendor of the land of dreams.

USELESS

No use trying, restless friend,
   To buy all that's in the store,
If you did they'd simply send
   Orders straightway for some more.

No use thinking, festive one,
   You can drink the great world dry,
Vines will grow and presses run,
   Pouring forth a new supply.

No use hoping, reverend sage,
   To learn all the world can teach,
Time rolls on and every age
   Brings new wisdom into reach.

No use trying to compel
   Life to yield more than its due.
You have done exceeding well,
   If your small share comes to you.

MAN AND HIS PHILOSOPHIES

Philosophers in every day,
   As well as every land,
Have been compelled to pause and say,
   "I do not understand."

And one of them will weep because
   Mankind seems in distress.
Another laughs and claims applause
   For his light-heartedness.

In common purpose for awhile
   Opposing minds draw near;
The wit who greets us with a smile,
   The poet with a tear.

A HUMBLE APPRECIATION

You 'preciate the people who when sorrow comes our
    way,
Come 'round to sympathize and know jes' what's polite
    to say.
There is others, too, whose voices aren't very often heard;
In fact, they lend a helpin' hand an' never say a word,
'Cause now an' then you find a friend that seems to know
    the way
To help you an' jes' does it an' there ain't no words to say.
Kind words are more than coronets. You value them a
    lot;
But how you love the feller that was "Johnny on the spot!"

I don't approve of slang, but every now an' then you see
Some phrase that tells the story like it re'ly ought to be.
You feel an admiration for the wisdom that is shown
In pointin' out your error, after all your cash has flown.
The good advice he gives you is an article that's prime,
The only difficulty is he wasn't there on time.
But the feller that you cling to, who will never be forgot,
Is the one who jes' said nothin', but was "Johnny on
    the spot."

NO SUCH THING

There's no such thing as "down an' out."
Folks don't know what they're talkin' 'bout
When they throw up their hands an' say,
"There's no more luck to come my way."
As long as you have hands to toil,
There's food to gather from the soil.
As long as you have ears to hear,
There's somethin' worth your learnin' near.
While you possess a voice to speak,
There's some one who your words will seek.
There's disappointment an' there's doubt,
But no such thing as "down an' out."

THE CRUEL JEST

In days gone by, the king would choose
   Some strange misshapen creature, who
By his misfortune might amuse
The courtiers for an hour or two.
They looked upon him undismayed,
   And 'round the board the laughter went
To see a being who had strayed
   So far from Nature's fair intent.

En-throned Reason now takes heed,
   Not of the mold, but of the mind.
That suave or snarling thing called Greed
   Makes mirth for those to sport inclined.
We deck some policy of shame
   With Cap and bells, and bravely keep
Our sneers, and play the cynic's game
   And laugh when we might better weep.

THE LAST WORD

Though mighty be the wisdom that is shown
As wise men know they have still wiser grown,
There is a power mightier than them all
Which must claim heed forever to its call.

It is not the command of gilded pride,
Nor martial force, which cannot be denied,
That keeps us waiting still in hope to find
A way of benefit to human kind.

And, though dull force may seek to dominate
With promises and threats among the great,
Heard with authority that must endure
Are voices of the children and the poor.

[29]

FATHER TIME

We all know a fellow called Old Father Time.
He has taught us in prose; he has frivoled in rhyme.
One day he will give us a song or a laugh
And the next he is writing a short epitaph.
The way he jogs on is so quietly queer
We seldom remember his presence so near.
But he measures our steps as we falter or climb.
He keeps tab on us all, does this Old Father Time.

But his hand is so gentle, although it is strong,
That he helps us a lot as he leads us along.
And the ruins that rise on the hills of the past
He covers with ivy and roses at last.
He teaches the smiles of the present to glow,
While the sorrows are left to the long, long ago.
And the knell turns to joy in its merriest chime—
He's a pretty good fellow, is Old Father Time.

THE BOY AND THE SUNBEAM

"I am washing my face in the sunshine,"
    Said the baby who played on the floor,
Where a great shaft of light through the window
    Of gold spread its generous store.
"I'm washing my face in the sunshine"
    He laughed in his innocent glee;
And the wee sturdy chap made a picture
    'Twere well worth a journey to see.

The mother bent over and loved him
    As only a mother knows how;
And she whispered a prayer as she kissed him:
    "May it be with you ever as now.
May you turn to the sky and its shining,
    Till the journey before you is done,
A face that is honest and happy
    And bathed in the light of the sun!"

GREATNESS

A wise man said: "I shall disdain
The little things of life so vain;
I shall not waste my thoughtful power
On what may fade as fades the flower.

"The sun in his majestic sway
Directs the planets far away.
'Tis thus that I my joy shall find
Remote, with trifles left behind."

And then a bud to blossom came,
The wise man's face grew flushed with shame.
He murmured: "How hast thou replied
Unto my folly and my pride!

"That monarch of the universe,
With might to shatter and coerce,
Doth gently color, as he glows,
The petal of the fragile rose!"

THE SIGNAL

Be patient with the cap and bells.
    The garb is humble as a rule,
Yet loyal service often dwells
    Beneath the guise of ridicule.

It is when Fate appears to jest
    And lets a folly thrive too long
That tragedy, with cruel zest,
    For Right is substituting Wrong.

So patient be with Punchinel,
    Who bids us taste before we quaff.
And as of danger he would tell
    Sends forth the signal of a laugh.

MEMORY MISMANAGED

The things that we remember
  Will too often cause a sigh
That brings flame into the ember
  Of a grievance long gone by.

We recall the bitter speeches
  That impulsively were made
And the old mistake that teaches
  While far better lessons fade.

Generous kindness seems to perish
  As we harbor vain regret
And the memories we cherish
  Are the things we should forget.

A FROMAGE FANTASY

A tiny bit of Camembert!
What strange illusions linger there!
What visions direful and distressed
Through hours that should be sweet with rest!

Who'd think that 'neath your creamy guise
The sting of nitric acid lies,
Or that you could such pictures draw
More strange than Dante ever saw.

As mildly white as melting snow
You are, alas to those who know,
More potent than the weirdest drop
That ever left a chemist's shop.

Compared with you how trifling seems
The source of Monte Cristo's dreams
Both hemp and poppy fail to share
Your mystic might, oh, Camembert.

ALL IN VAIN

While musing on the rights of man
    And wealth of nations,
I think upon my boyhod plan;
    No decorations
Bade me a doubtful claim assert
    To legal tender;
I needed just my pants, a shirt
    And one suspender.
Why now do men bewail the price
    Of gilded splendor,
And gamblers win with loaded dice
    More legal tender?
Why does my envy of them hurt
    When these could render
My life content—just pants, a shirt
    And one suspender?

THE WAYSIDE

Someone's got to work to let
    Some other fellow play;
Just a few can hope to get
    A constant holiday;
Some in autos skim the ground
    A merry pace they strike
And some must haul the gravel 'round
    To level up the pike.

Some with careless songs and jokes
    Can gaily glide about
And some must be wheelbarrow folks
    To smooth the pathway out;
But if it's toil or just a game
    That gives this life its zest;
We all get weary just the same
    And thankful for a rest.

NOTHING NEW

The cynic vows, with bitter tongue,
"Some day the songs will all be sung,
This world of ours at last we'll view
Bereft of everything that's new!"
In sooth, Sir Cynic, don't you know
That all this happened long ago?
The breeze which through the hedges swept
Where savage loves their trysting kept
In days primeval, did inspire
The love song of the heart's desire,
And when a rival met his fate
The song of triumph and of hate
That still resounds in martial tones
Was intermingled with his groans.
The songs of wedding and of feast,
The songs of penitent and priest,
Are echoings from far away
In some remote ancestral day.
For other songs we strive in vain,
We can but sing these o'er again.

PEACE

For Peace we Pray. The Years that fade—
Each seeks life's tumult to evade.
Each Year, as it has dawned, has found
The clouds of hatred gathering 'round.

If Peace shall mean the idle mind
To sympathy no more inclined,
The loitering ease that takes no heed
Of fellow men who dwell in need.

If Peace shall mean a place secure,
Where men unwillingly endure
While Envy clashes with Disdain,
For Peace we'll Pray, and Pray in vain.

THE DIPLOMAT

Spite of all the churlish chatter,
  It is quite a serious matter
To become a proper guardian of the peace.
  You must have a disposition
  That would fit you for a mission
To Turkey or the Balkans or to Greece.
  You must treat the children kindly,
  And when people jostle blindly
At a crowded crossing 'mid the dust and noise,
  You must grab a perfect stranger
  And convey him out of danger
In a way that won't disturb his equipoise.

  You must learn the regulations,
  And likewise the laws of nations,
To avoid the chance of diplomatic jar.
  You must listen uncomplaining,
  All your sense of mirth restraining,
While they come to tell you what their troubles are.
  You should have a fund of knowledge,
  More than could be learned at college,
To assist each weary wanderer in distress.
  And your compensation should be
  All a bank director's could be—
Though I fancy it's considerably less!

THE UNLUCKY INVENTOR

Could you a mouse trap make, oh friend,
  Surpassing all the rest,
Unto your door would lines extend
  Of those who seek the best.
And it might prove the same old joke
  Of which you've often heard.
Some profited, while you went broke
  On mouse trap stock preferred.

[35]

THE WARRIOR

Primeval man was all untaught
  And crude of manners as of speech.
He made himself a club and fought
  The foe that strayed within his reach.
He fought for shelter or for food,
  He fought to conquer or to die.
He loved his own, though fierce his mood,
  And when he fought he well knew why.

As time has marched, the bugle note
  Resounds instead of nature's growl.
Resplendent banners proudly float,
  Where wild men once were wont to prowl.
The battle is a fearful show.
  Primeval man was rude and grim,
But when he met and slew a foe
  He knew just why he hated him.

REGRET

"Didn't mean to make the trouble!"
  That's the cry o'er damage done;
"Didn't know the thing was loaded;
  Didn't mean to shoot the gun.
Didn't mean to start the story
  That I thought was such a joke,
'Til it made so much confusion—
  Kind 'o sorry that I spoke."

How deliberate intentions
  Mock us as they go astray,
While some trifling inadvertence
  Shifts our lives from day to day.
Make your lofty resolutions,
  Do your best to see 'em through,
And achievement yet may conquer
  Things you didn't mean to do.

JOYOUS AWAKENING

One night I dreamt I was a King
Or Emperor or some such thing,
And sat upon a gilded throne
And spoke up in a haughty tone,
While courtiers knelt and flattered me.
And when I jested, laughed with glee,
And trembled, lest I might, some day,
Chop off their heads or stop their pay.
Another King came drifting nigh
He was a crude and husky guy.
The way he bluffed me was a shame,
He showed me where to sign my name.
He did not hesitate to scoff;
He showed me just where I got off.
Stenographers next flouted me,
My minstrels all sang off the key,
And when I traveled forth in state
Some Anarchist would lie in wait,
Who aimed at me, and then got hissed,
By former friends, because he missed—
Oh, welcome sound! Oh, sweet relief!
The Old Alarm Clock ends my grief.
Take back the scepter and the crown!
Just lead me to my job downtown!

ANOTHER GUESS

"What is the difference," again we say,
    'Twixt statesmanship and politics precarious
As this great world goes rolling on its way
    With methods open-minded or nefarious.
The question often makes our pulses throb,
    There seems to be no hope of getting through with it.
The politician knows the way to land a job;
    The statesman tries to tell him what to do with it.

IKEY

Have you seen "Little Ikey?"—the child of the curb,
  The wandering elf with the big, dark eyes,
Whose calm self-possession no shock can disturb;
  Who laughs at the world he so bravely defies.
With a face that is dirty, a cap that is torn
  And breeches whose buttons have wandered away,
You may meet him at night or at earliest morn,
  A somebody's baby, somehow gone astray.

How well has he measured the mood of the throng,
  The throng that brings pennies to Ikey's small mart;
That welcomes the mummer who babbles a song
  And buffets the creature who cries from his heart.
There is pathos indeed in his ribald refrain;
  And yet, his child-nature must suffer no scar.
He is only the echo that mocks us again;
  The mirror that shows men the things that they are.

How slight are the weapons with which he sets out
  To fight for his life in the lists of the town.
Yet skill ever comes to the heart that is stout
  And ready to laugh at adversity's frown.
Beware bonnie wee ones, in pillowed repose,
  Whose cradles are swung where the kindly hours fly;
The future for you some defeats may disclose
  At the hands of the waif who must conquer or die.

THE RESULT

If everybody told the truth
  And ne'er indulged in yarns grotesque,
This world would be improved, forsooth,
  But nothing like so picturesque.

[38]

OLYMPICS

Backward we turn and endeavor to learn
   Some facts of the deeds and the names
Who for spirited sessions would meet and adjourn
   In the early Olympian Games.
Aphrodite no doubt from the sea would come out
   As a swimmer of wonderful grace;
And had baseball been known, all the public would
      shout,
   As Zeus made a slide for first base.

Aethiopians proud would bring cheers long and loud
   As they leaped in a marvelous style.
Dionysus would come to serve drinks to the crowd
   With a slightly effeminate smile;
A race, you'll agree, would be thrilling to see
   And the prizes would surely amaze.
Olympics are not what they once seemed to be
   In the old hoss and chariot days.

PAVED WITH PRECIOUS YEARS

There are roads out to the ocean
   Where the dashing waters shine,
Others to the storm's commotion
   Range above the timber line!
There are roads for homeward travel.
   There is one which ever seems
A bright journey to unravel
   To the castle of our dreams.

While the roads we must be building
   For the toiler's simple need,
This one we are gayly gilding
   With the hopes we love to heed.
Costs attend upon our scheming,
   Be it great or be it small,
But the highway of our dreaming
   Is most costly of them all.

MENTAL PHENOMENA

A most successful man was he;
  His mental gifts were great.
And yet the tricks his mind would play
  Were strange to contemplate.
He once gave out an interview,
  'Twas criticized a lot;
Next morning half the things he said
  He totally forgot.
Which shows the finest intellect
  May now and then be incorrect.

He ran a business that controlled
  Most of the world's affairs.
And yet, when the grand jury met
  And took him unawares
The wondrous mind that in finance
  Achieved the highest rank
When questioned on the witness stand
  Became a total blank.
Which proves the theory, more or less
  That geniuses are hard to guess.

COVERING

"What does it matter what we wear?"
Some persons venture to declare
Though startled by a mode of dress
That makes a garment less and less.
But when mentalities you see
From ornament entirely free,
Parading boldly, on display,
We gaze with feelings far from gay.
And though a slightness of attire
We tolerate—perhaps admire—
Embarrassment you'll surely find
If caught with nothing on your mind!

I'M THE BROTHER
OF A HUNDRED GIRLS OR SO

I often sit and ponder
On the girls away back yonder
In Memory Land, where all the girls were fair.
I can recollect them clearly,
Some I married, very nearly,
For they smiled on me and really seemed to care.
But we kissed and then we parted.
I was often broken hearted
As in turn they said in accents sweet and low:
"My affection, dear, is due you.
I will be a sister to you"—
I'm the brother of a hundred girls or so!

My broken heart soon mended.
Recovery was splendid,
As I smiled into another face so calm.
Now a hundred husbands greet me.
They are always glad to meet me;
And a hundred children call me "Uncle Tom."
Though I've missed the blissful station
Of a marital relation,
I am competent to give advice, I know,
On the methods of expression
Mingling fervor with discretion.
I'm the brother of a hundred girls or so.

NO COURT PRESENTATION

I may not go to see the king.
I dare not call upon the queen.
To them I cannot say a thing
To mar their dignity serene.
I leave them to their gloom so rich.
I dare not make it disappear,
Although I know some stories which
I'd really like to have them hear!

[41]

A RUSTIC PHILOSOPHER

I ain't in the swim,
  An' my chances is slim
To shine with the fortunate crowd.
  But the leaves 'neath the tree
  Is a-laughin' with glee,
An' their laughter ain't vulgar nor loud.
  An' the loiterin' stream,
  With its ripple an' gleam,
Is singin' a comfortin' song.
  It's considerable fun
  Jes' to sit in the sun
An' watch the ol' world move along.
  There's an echo afar
  Of the bustle an' jar
Where the struggle's relentless an' cold;
  I miss the acclaim
  That's accorded to fame,
But, in spite of ambitions gone wrong,
  It's considerable fun
  Jes' to sit in the sun
An' watch the ol' world move along.

THE FINAL QUESTION

'Mongst all the prophets and the creeds
That measure up our thoughts and deeds,
Each will at last apply this test:
"Oh, Mortal, have you done your best?"

If you have missed the joy intense
That comes to glorious excellence,
You still will claim an honored rest
If you have simply done your best!

JEWELS

A weary woman paused to tend
  The flowers near the cottage door;
And to each blossom seemed a friend,
  Who learned to love them more and more.

"I have no gems," she gently sighed,
  "Yet gems I truly crave no less
Than yon fair lady in the pride
  Of her luxurious loveliness.

"But these bright blossoms gleaming fair,
  Which simple love and toil secure,
Reflecting colors rich and rare—
  These are the jewels of the poor."

KEEPING FAITH

Some little child looks up to you
  As one of wisdom's very great,
A guide and teacher good and true,
  A shield from any adverse fate.
We may suspect that he is wrong.
  Let us give battle to each foe,
And try to be both big and strong
  For love of those who trust us so.

MEMORY SONG

A gentle song came through the air.
  Its words were fair indeed,
And yet the melody so rare
  Was all I paused to heed.
The poem that its rhymes unfold
  Remained to me unknown,
The tenderest stories that it told
  Were memories of my own.

THE STAR OF HOPE

High in the heavens shines a star
  Whose speed no mortal eye can guess.
We gaze upon it from afar
  And marvel at its loveliness.

A star of prophecy it seems,
  In the deep silence of the night,
To hail fulfillment of the dreams
  Which have been beautiful and bright.

It is the airmail on its way
  That sends to us this radiant glow;
It has its message to convey
  To all who wonder here below.

It bears the evidence of will
  And power that will never cease;
To labor, not for martial skill
  But for earth's promised love and peace.

THE STAND-BY

Some friends are like the roses sweet
  That bloom when summer warms the air;
With gentle smiling to complete
  A scene that is already fair.
    But when the wintry skies are gray
    Alack, the roses fade away!

And some are like the holly bough,
  With thorny leaf and stalwart mien,
Whose rugged touch would wound the brow
  Of pleasure in a summer scene.
    But when the winter frowns severe
    The holly bough is stanch with cheer.

THE LONG ROAD

Traveling on through Sorrowland; traveling day by day.
Traveling to Tomorrowland that is never far away.
Traveling for the beauty where the twilight country
    gleams.
It looks so very near, yet it's much farther than it seems.

There's many a fragile blossom that may cheer us as we go.
But the briar lurks to pierce us and the road is steep and
    slow.
Some great mysterious promise of beatitude and rest
Keeps us ever striving onward, keeps us hoping for the
    best.

THE TIRED CHILD

Though puppets come with flaxen poll
    And gleaming eyes of luster deep,
At night we find the old rag doll
    Enfolded in her arms asleep.

And so, as through the years we rove
    And sometimes thrive in fortune's quest,
The ones whom first we learned to love
    Are still the ones we love the best.

A FLOWER

I love the flower not so much
    For all its beauty passing rare,
As for the hand whose tender touch
    Has brought it near with loving care.

EQUAL DISTRIBUTION

A boy in a school was a rather bad boy,
  Though his mother would never admit it.
In mischief his time he would often employ
  And they couldn't persuade him to quit it.
When punishment came he admitted no blame,
  But mentioned life's plots as they thicken;
He merely remarked it was all in the game,
  It was his turn for takin' a lickin'.

He tried to be good; did the best that he could;
  He'd listen to erudite speeches
Of things passed around with a plan understood
  As one which equality teaches.
"I have laughed," he declared, "when the pleasure I
    shared,
  With sorrow why should I be stricken,
And let my sad spirit be caught unprepared
  When it's my turn for takin' a lickin'."

VARIETY OF PRISONERS

How oft on history's page we view
  Great plans that fail;
For scientists, and martyrs, too,
  Have gone to jail!

Awakening comes to brightest dreams
  Whose colors fail.
Philosophers with splendid schemes
  Have gone to jail.

Upon the vast array we look
  Where men sought bail,
And even here and there a crook
  Has gone to jail!

A PROUD POSSESSOR

I know a queer monopolist. You never get a chance
  To tell your hard luck story when he's busy with his
      own.
He never notices the flowers. He never gives a glance
  At all the bits of beauty which into each path are
      thrown.
He does not boast of hoarded gold nor of his bonds nor
      stocks.
  He even says his interest in life is rather small.
He never talks of treasure guarded safe by bolts and locks.
  But when it comes to troubles—why he thinks he has
      them all!

We're all collectors in a plain or scientific way;
  Some gather mighty dollars; some are hunting butter-
      flies;
Some seek for wisdom; others are alert for stories gay.
  And some are always busy just collecting tears and
      sighs.
He's gloomy, but superior, when with my tale of woe
  In search of human sympathy on him I chance to call.
He doesn't brag of riches nor of power to make a show,
  But when it comes to troubles—why he thinks he has
      them all.

AGE LIMITS

There is a man who perseveres
To learn his business through the years
And when he really "knows his stuff"
They hand him out a chill rebuff
And say "give way to flaming youth
Which claims the privilege, in sooth
Of smoking cigarettes between
Kegs in a powder magazine!"

UNBELIEF

I saw a face in public print.
It wore a frown; it had a squint.
Its lip was curled into a sneer.
Its eyelids hung with sullen leer.
Its nose was twisted and its scowls
Were like those of the wolf that prowls.
I had to go and meet this man.
I shuddered and I almost ran
In terror from his lurking place.
I feared to view that awful face.
And then a voice that did not jar
Said, "Pray, sit down!   Have a cigar!"
I looked him squarely in the eye.
I did not quail and seek to fly.
He was a patient, kindly man,
With features on the usual plan;
Of simple mien and friendly mood
And never an intention rude.
I may believe the things they say
By voice or print from day to day.
But never in a thousand moons
Will I believe those flip cartoons!

PAGLIACCI

Perhaps at me you sneer,
    My dear,
Because I'm only just a clown,
    Whose antics, often queer,
    Appear
At moments to amuse the town.
    But if my heart sincere
    Can cheer
And from your brow efface a frown,
    Your smile so frank and clear,
    My dear,
Means more than stateliest renown.

DESERVING OF CONSIDERATION

Bow to the boast of the self-made man
Defying nature in all its plan!
The oak ere it grows to its sturdy height
Depends on the soil and the rain and light;
The river that flows to the mighty deep
Is fed by the streams on the hillside steep;
The flower that blooms and the ripening grain,
Were the sun shut out, would reach forth in vain,
And the cubs in the wildest creature's lair
Would die in a lack of sheltering care.
But the self-made man apart doth dwell,
The work of some strange, spontaneous spell,
With never a memory in his mind
Of help in the days that are left behind;
No friendly hint when the luck ran slow,
No timely aid when the cash was low.
He has missed a lot in the strife and stress
Where he conquers in splendid loneliness.
Let him claim such happiness as he can—
Defer to the boast of the self-made man!

BACK AFTER A LONG TIME

The Big Chief tossed his boomerang,
    That weapon of the long ago,
While wild admiring songs they sang
    Wherever crowds beheld the show.

It came back with an awful bang
    And set the heavens all aglow
As planes and bombs that fiercely rang
    And mercilessly laid him low.

THE CRUSTY OLD FELLOW

"Crusty old fellow," they used to say,
As they watched him cautiously make his way
Into the vault where the bars and locks
Stoutly guarded his treasure box.
"Crusty old fellow, who loves to gloat
Over certificate, coin and note—
Counting them with a long caress
Worthy a lover's tenderness!"

He heard them not as he passed them by
With shuffling step and with furtive eye;
The lines of his face were hard and cold
As if he had been all his lifetime old;
Old and wary and far too wise
To yield to the laughter of youthful eyes.
Careless of comment good or bad,
Old and wary, and, somehow, sad.

Into the strong room he made his way,
His treasure box open before him lay;
And he looked again, to be assured
That the door behind him was well secured;
Then laid out papers, where written bold
Were solemn compacts to pay him gold.
Some of them debts—'tis strange, but true—
Uncollected, though long since due.

With trembling fingers he then unwinds
The faded ribbon that loosely binds
A packet, and counts with a miser's care
The letters lying before him there.
And he fondly touches some little thing
Like a handkerchief or a plain gold ring,
Or the miniature of a sweet-faced girl,
Or a withered flower, or a golden curl.

And his face in the twilight's softening glow
Grew sweet with the smiling of long ago.
But scarce had he given the key a turn,

His lips compressed and his eye grew stern.
And they said with a sneer, "How he loves to gloat
Over certificate, coin and note,
Counting them with a long caress
Worthy a lover's tenderness!"

"IT CAN'T BE DONE"

The man who misses all the fun
Is he who says "It can't be done!"
In solemn pride he stands aloof
And greets each venture with reproof.
Had he the power, he'd efface
The history of the human race;
We'd have no steam nor motor cars,
No streets lit by electric stars;
No telegraph nor telephone.
We'd linger in the age of stone,
Where when some keen barbaric brain
Of life's conditions dared complain,
And planned a wheel on which to roll
The load his arms could not control,
Sneers rose from all the mighty crew
That ever scoffs at what is new.
The world would sleep if things were run
By men who say, "It can't be done!"

DEPTH

"My thought is deep," the grave man said;
"So do not be by folly led,
And strive my meaning to pursue.
My thought is far too deep for you."
Then said the simple passerby:
"Your thought is deep, I can't deny.
It lies secure from common wit,
Because 'neath words you've buried it."

VIGILS

He's a picture for a painter
  As he's lying fast asleep;
Naught is prettier nor quainter
  Than the dimples as they creep
'Round his little cheeks so rosy;
He's as dainty as a posy
In the little crib so cozy
  Where he's lying fast asleep.

And the moonbeams pause to love him
  As he's lying fast asleep;
And the stars that shine above him
  Tender vigils seem to keep.
And the smile so softly beaming
Back in answer to their gleaming
Tell of angels in his dreaming
  As he's lying fast asleep.

All is snowlike in its whiteness
  Where he's lying fast asleep,
And you step with all the lightness
  Of the shadows as they creep,
Lest the slight ties he might sever
And float far off and forever
From the world of rude endeavor
  While he's lying fast asleep.

TRUTH IN THE WELL

Truth is at the bottom of a well.
We toil to bring her up, so legends tell,
But she is weary and alas, all wet.
We look upon her plight with great regret,
She is sad company. So with disdain
We pick her up and throw her back again.

LITTLE BOY SLEEPYHEAD

Little boy sleepyhead twilight is falling
  And shadows are gathering near,
To you, from out yonder your dream friends are calling,
  While I stand in loneliness here.

I gaze on your face where smiles quietly hover,
  As soft as the moonlight that gleams,
And I wish that some way your fond heart could discover,
  To give me a share in your dreams.

Little boy sleepyhead days would be dreary,
  Except for the thinking of you
And many a night has been watchful and weary
  While waiting for daybreak anew.

But my hand will be strong and my heart will grow bolder,
  With every bright morning that gleams,
If some day you will nestle your head on my shoulder
  And give me a share in your dreams.

ONLY ONE LOVE

A brook from the mountain came flowing
  He sang to the blossoms he passed on his way
I shall find 'neath the skies crystal glowing
  The ocean eternal some day.

There's only one ocean forever.
  There's only one sky up above.
There's only one lifetime, my darling,
  In life there is only one love.

I have wandered afar, scarcely knowing
  The pathway that fate bade me swiftly pursue,
Yet I knew like the brook gently flowing,
  Some day I should find love and you.

[53]

A MEMORY

The world will be the same, they say,
  When you and I and all have done
Our various tasks as best we may,
  And then departed one by one.

The world will be the same. The sky
  Now gleaming bright, then overcast;
And blossoms will delight the eye
  Anew, then wither in the blast.

The shout of hope, the moan of fear,
  The empty jest, the idle song,
The gentle word, the cynic sneer,
  Will still go echoing through the throng.

And yet as the farewells are said
  In voice, in silence or in tears,
A subtle, saddening change is spread
  And faster speed the hurrying years.

The clasp of reassuring hands,
  The sound of a familiar tone,
Far more than sky or blossoming lands
  Make up the world that we have known.

When only recollections fill
  The haunts that loved ones have made sweet,
It is a world of beauty still;
  And yet transformed and incomplete.

INVOLUNTARY CONTRIBUTION

Great men who once led the Nation,
  After many years have fled
Often stand in an oration
  For some things they never said.

[54]

ONE OF THE WORTHY

Oh, the man with sweet-voiced violin
   Is a wizard whose delicate wand
Shuts out all the world with its heartless din
   And transports us to wonderland.
And the man with the brush makes the colors blend
   In a glory that never fails.
And yet in the end we must all depend
   On the man with the hammer and nails.

The pen may plod and ink may flow
   Through precept and prayer and proof,
But we yearn, perforce, when the bleak winds blow
   To the builder of wall and roof.
Here's to artist and scholar and soldier, too,
   As each toward fame's summit scales,
And a tribute in passing—'tis sure his due—
   To the man with the hammer and nails!

PROCRASTINATION

"There's plenty of time," said the morning sun,
   As he laughed in the rosy sky—
So I smiled at the task that was still undone
   And the hours went drifting by.

And the day grew short and the shadows long—
   And the moon with the silvery beam
Taught the breeze to whisper the same old song,
   "There is plenty of time to dream."

The clock is in contradiction set
   As it rings with a careless chime—
The hours are too short for the task—and yet
   There is always "plenty of time."

[55]

SAYS UNCLE JIM

Says my Uncle Jim, in a serious tone,
"Sometimes it is best to let bygones alone;
Apologies ought to be made when they're due,
When sincerity calls, and they ought to be few.
Sometimes such an eloquent style they'll provide
They almost seem like they were pointin' with pride;
Your own self-approval is what you must win
As you solemnly vow 'not to do it ag'in!'"

"Remorse is no good if it's told in a way
Like that of an actor rehearsing a play.
He may take an encore despite your advice;
Your scolding he likes 'cause you do it so nice.
It's upon your own conscience that you must rely
For a record that may be approved by and by.
A fine explanation seems shabby and thin
Unless you resolve 'not to do it ag'in.'"

WARNING

Though ignorance is never bliss,
    Despite what poets say,
Of wisdom it were well to miss
    Too constant a display.
For pride, as people all agree,
    Oft goes before a fall,
So pause, and do not seek to be
    The man who knows it all.

E'en though all knowledge you have won
    Of things both old and new,
You'll merely be so good that none
    Can think that you are true.
For up amid the frosty heights
    You'll stray beyond recall,
And pass your lonely days and nights—
    The man who knows it all.

DECEPTIVE

The overly wise men were baffled one day,
  Their faces showed signs of distress.
"A man has rushed into affairs," murmured they
  "Whose methods nobody can guess.
We credited him as we'd darkly surmise,
  With cunning well worthy of dread;
We discounted his words and we find with surprise
  That he really meant all that he said!"

You can see through the play that is made by a knave;
  You can cope now and then with a fool.
'Tis easy to fathom the people who crave
  Success 'neath hypocrisy's rule.
But candor is something so new in the game
  That even the cleverest head
Is baffled and maybe left drooping in shame
  By the man who meant all that he said.

DREAMS

He dreamt of castles in the air
  That rose with stately grace.
Where gallant men and women fair
  Were garbed in silks and lace.
He dreamt of homage claimed by fear.
  He saw himself supreme.
The humbled hordes with gifts drew near—
  And it was but a dream.

Again he dreamt—of house enough
  To shelter love and toil;
Of friends who helped o'er journeys rough,
  And of a generous soil
Where industry might find its share
  Of good, when work was through,
And song and laughter filled the air—
  And then his dreams came true.

PROTEST

"I hate this talk," said Plodding Pete,
  "Of sending millionaires to jail.
They'll have the cells fixed up so neat
  That steady customers will fail
To recognize the place where they
Have often passed a quiet day.

"They'll have electric lights strung 'round
  And fancy rugs upon the floor;
They'll cook up t'ings whose names will sound
  Like food we never ate before.
It will be worth a fellow's life
To get caught eatin' with a knife!

"There'll be such style around the place
  A-caterin' to folks like those,
You'll want to go an' hide your face
  Unless you've brought your evening clothes—
Let's have one spot where money kings
Can't come around a-runnin' things!"

THE TRAVELER

The world goes swiftly spinning on through space,
  And 'mongst the passengers the lucky chaps
Get comfortable seats, each to his place;
  But most of us are hanging to the straps.

ELABORATION

The bird that sings up in the tree
    Exclaimed "I see I have no chance;
If I a modern hit would be
    I've got to learn a funny dance."

[58]

MR. SPEAKER!

I am waiting while I labor for my place there in the fray;
I am waiting for the chance to show just why I draw
    my pay.
Great thoughts are mine—they oft surprise me by their
    lavishness—
They're rapidly evolved, but not so easy to express.
I conquer my impatience as I think upon the prize
Which visions of the future brings so fair before my eyes.
I am waiting, simply waiting, 'til at last it comes my turn
To holler "Mr. Speaker!" or "I move that we adjourn!"

I listen to the wisdom that comes dropping from the lip
Of each patriotic prophet, of each seer of statesmanship.
I listen to the speeches, for I may not yet presume
To penetrate the secrets of the big committee room.
But studious application brings its sure reward in time,
So I read the economic lore of every age and clime,
In hopes that I by staunch determination yet may learn
To holler "Mr. Speaker!" or "I move that we adjourn!"

DISCONCERTING

Important indeed are the forms of our speech
    And a vast disappointment we know
In the things we are striving to learn or to teach
    When a "yes man" forgets and says "no."

PRUDENT RETICENCE

Oh, he who babbles with a will
    May find his credit shrinking.
'Tis often better to keep still
    And make folks think you're thinking.

PUTTING IT OVER

A great economist am I.
  Whene'er I make a speech
To demonstrate I always try
  How far a thought may reach.
If loud the voice is made to ring
  In phrases fine and fit,
A very ordinary thing
  Will oftimes make a hit.

Let India rubber be your guide
  In literary style;
The method carefully applied
  Will cause success to smile
On your endeavors. 'Tisn't hard.
  Strive on, and do not flinch
To do your talking by the yard
  And thinking by the inch.

LIFE HAS BECOME A SERIOUS MATTER

I much deplore the hours that I misplace
In studying ads that might improve my face.
I know I'd nearly perish with regret
If the wrong tooth paste I should chance to get,
And break into an agonizing scream
If I went wrong in buying shaving cream!

DEFINITION

If you the definition ask
  Of that small word "mistake"
It's something quite mysterious
  That other people make.

A CONGRESSIONAL OCCURRENCE

His mind sped forth to other things
  When first he made a speech;
His fancy, with erratic wings,
  Flew far beyond his reach.
He paused and stammered dismally,
  And when he'd gotten through,
His mind was naught but vacancy—
  The hall was emptying, too.

But when his fond constituents came
  The Record's page to scan,
Where, well revised and not the same,
  His rhetoric smoothly ran,
They cheered his name, both high and low,
  And the assurance passed
That that back number, Cicero,
  Had found his match, at last.

AN ORATOR MAKES GOOD

He said at the first he had nothing to say.
  His manner was quite overbearing.
We thought by his vastly superior way
  He must have some thoughts worth declaring.
At last to the microphone forward he went,
  With platitudes lengthy he fed it.
It was done, all agreed, with a kindly intent.
  He had nothing to say—and he said it.

It was when he was cautious and feared that the crowd
  Might fail to accord him politeness,
But he soon learned to offer his eloquence proud
  On the world and its wrongness or rightness.
He stepped right along with a voice that was strong—
  That mike—he long since ceased to dread it.
His vocalization boomed forth like a song.
  He had nothing to say—and he said it.

[61]

THE COUNTRY POLITICIAN

If there's any public question that you fail to see quite
    through,
Jes' drop aroun' some time an' I'll explain 'em all to you.
I've studied an' I've figgered till I've got the bottom facks
'Bout this League of Nation's business an' likewise the
    income tax.
I never held no office. But mine ain't the only case
When a thinker an' a speaker failed to git the highest place.
All through the history of the world examples you will see
Like Dan'l Webster, Henry Clay, an' James G.
    Blaine—an' me.

It's hard to find sech orators as flourished long ago.
Your colleges can't make 'em; they have simply got to
    grow.
I have spoken fer my party jes' the very best I knew—
But the other feller allus gits the 'p'intments when we're
    through.
My coat's a little shiny an' my feet kin feel the air.
But those men didn't keer fer style. They hadn't time
    to spare.
They spoke up bold an' fearless; an' I wish that more
    would be
Like Dan'l Webster, Henry Clay, an' James G.
    Blaine—an' me.

There's no use of repinin' an' the nation ain't to blame
Ef it sometimes makes a discord when it blows the trump
    o' fame.
There's no use of complainin' ef they happen to fergit
An' place the laurel wreath upon a brow it doesn't fit.
Time always finds occasion—it was never known to slip—
To show the men that labored in their true relationship.
A few will be remembered through the centuries that
    flee,
Like Dan'l Webster, Henry Clay, an' James G.
    Blaine—an' me.

An' would you say that one whom future nations must
    admire,
Because he's out o' work has missed life's loftiest desire?
Shall he be envious of the man who, countin' up his pelf,
Exclaims, "I loved my country, but I hustled fer myself!"
The present generation may fergit your thought an' toil,
But they're seeds which you have planted here in fame's
    eternal soil.
An' the fruits are fruits of honor. Men will sing from
    sea to sea
'Bout Dan'l Webster, Henry Clay, an' James G.
    Blaine—an' me!

It's a cup of cheer an' troubles that the glory seeker begs.
It's nectar while it bubbles, but it's wormwood at dregs.
So I do my little duty an' I thank my little star
That my various disapp'intments ain't no wuss than what
    they are.
I think, when I'm reminded of the way my life was spent,
Of other people who was right, though never President,
And it needs sech unpaid workers fer to keep the country
    free
As Dan'l Webster, Henry Clay, James G. Blaine—an' me.

PARTING COMPANY

A man whose hair was white as snow
Was telling boys the way to go.

His early life was not so good,
He skinned his neighbors when he could.

Said he, "Be honest, true and kind,
And so a great reward you'll find.

That way for heaven you will prepare—
You probably won't find me there."

[63]

INDEPENDENCE DAY

When those fleeting flaming glories
   Were displayed across the sky
In remembrance of the stories
   Of brave men in days gone by,
Then we thought of deeds of daring
   And of clear and steadfast minds
That had set the country faring
   Safe through the tempestuous winds.

Then we pondered on the toiling
   And the watches of the night;
Of the suffering and despoiling
   Braved in reverence of the right.
And each memory we cherish
   Shall not fade away and die,
Shall not be allowed to perish
   Like a rocket in the sky.

ACCORDING TO OUR LIGHTS

Ben Franklin brought the lightning down
Which now illuminates the town.
We don't employ this light to note
The words of wisdom that he wrote.
We squander it on a display
Of jazzy joy in circles gay.
But Lincoln, by the old pine knot,
Wrote words that cannot be forgot.

THE FACE ON THE STAMP

George Washington, whose face serene
Upon the postage stamp is seen,
Might sometimes lose his look of pride
If he knew what was mailed inside.

THE HERO

(Abraham Lincoln)

The sound of sorrow still reverberates
   As if the world were one great tolling bell
And everywhere a moving throng awaits
   In reverence as it hears the solemn knell.

The babel ceases for a little while
   And every language that mankind has known
Is hushed in mouths of innocence or guile
   It is a time for thought and thought alone.

He toiled for happiness and for repose
   To ease the paths that other men must tread,
But for himself the weary way he chose
   Lit by the stars eternal overhead.

The din again will rise—and every land
   Will name him and weave words of subtle art
And be perplexed—for few can understand
   The beating of a bold and generous heart.

LINCOLN'S BIRTHDAY

The clown stood humbly as he viewed
   The reverent emblems on display
Mid tributes of our gratitude
   To Lincoln on this honored day.

"He loved mankind with gentle zest,"
   Quoth he. "Life would be more worthwhile,
If I could but have framed a jest
   That might be worthy of his smile."

[65]

LOAFING ALONG

Ol' Father Time, he comes along,
    Wif a scythe an' a hour-glass too,
An' his wiskers a-growin' big an' strong
    An' his face a-lookin' blue.
He seem dat mounful dat I's skyart to look
In a almanac or a picture book
    As de days go rollin' by.

An' I says, "Father Time, it 'pears to me
    Dar's a better use foh sand
Dan a-runnin' it th'oo dat glass to see
    How dis life slips th'oo yoh hand.
De sand wuf puttin' dependence in
Is de kind dat he'ps you go in an' win
    As de days go rollin' by.

"You's a-standin' round' wif yoh eyes tear-dimmed
    A-loafin' an' lookin' sad.
If you'd spruce up mo' wif yoh whiskers trimmed.
    Dis worl' mightn't seem so bad.
But I never seen you make a pass
Wif you-all's scythe foh to cut no grass
    As de days go rollin' by.

So don' git mad if yoh photograph
    Is turned to de cabin wall.
We wants our chances to sing an' laugh
    An' you's tryin' to spoil 'em all,
A-mindin' us how de minutes go.
S'pos'n dey does! Dar's always mo'
    As de days go rollin' by."

VERSATILITY

I's done mos' ev'y kin' o' work; I useter drive a dray;
An' once I done kep' shovelin' coal clean through de
      blessed day.
I's lookin' foh experience, I's waitin' foh to git
A chance at sumpin' what I nebber ain't attempted yit.
I's follered up a mule along de towpath day by day;
I's druv a truck an' rassled wif de baggage on a dray;
But dar's jes' one occupation dat I thinks would suit my
      style—
I'd like to try a job o' millionairin' foh awhile.

Dey tells me dat's about de hardes' labor dat dar is.
But I bet it ain' sufficient to give me no rheumatiz.
I been a-cuttin' corn so much I reckons 'twould be
      strange
If I couldn' stan' de strain o' cuttin' coupons foh a change.
I doesn' ask foh idleness, I only wants to try
My han' at every kin' of work dat comes a-passin' by.
I merely names my preffunce, an' it ain' no cause to
      smile—
I'd like to try a job o' millionairin' foh awhile.

REMINDER

Be a little patient, chile! Dat's all you got to do!
By an' by a yaller flower will come a-peekin' through
Whah de leaves lay dead an' brown when autumn days
      were done—
Little yaller flower to tell you 'bout de summer sun!

Never mind de misty chill dat hovers roun' de do'!
We's had a heap o' June-time, an' we's gwinter hab some
      mo'.
Violets will tell you 'bout de summer skies so blue—
Be a little patient, chile! Dat's all you got to do!

MAY SONG

Wind come loafin' through de tree,
   An' sing a litle tune,
Singin' 'bout how long 'twill be
   Befo' we gits to June;
Singin' 'bout de bull frog and
   A-singin' 'bout de bird—
Dey's comin' 'long to jine de band,
   De finest ever heard;
Singin' 'bout de starlight mild,
   An' singin' 'bout de moon,
Singin' "Jes' keep patient, child;
   Dey's comin' pretty soon!"
Singin' 'bout de roses fair,
   'Bout mornin' glories, too,
A-spillin' sweetness on de air
   Dat soaks it through an' through.
It's got me hypnotized foh sho,
   It soun' so sweet to me,
Dat song de wind is singin' low
   Away up in de tree.

SO SOON

I wants you to step forward an' listen to me son.
When talkin' 'bout de doin's you's been an' gone an' done
Yoh calculations doesn't 'pear to hab a word to say
About de resolution dat you made on New Year Day.

You's figgerin' up de profit, an' you's figgerin' up de loss,
A-markin' down de prices an' a-countin' up de cos';
But I doesn't see no worriment a-lingerin' in yoh eye
Because you done discovered you's a resolution shy.

Take up yoh obligations, son, an' look de whole lot through,
An' don't confine yohself to bills an'notes dat's comin' due,
Get busy while de year is young befo' it seems too late;
Jes' take dat resolution book an' bring it up to date.

EXPECTATION

You's got to keep a-waitin'
  Wif a patience dat is strong,
'Case dar ain't no way o' statin'
  When its prime will come along.
But ebry time I sees it wif a fascinated eye
I know's it's gittin' bigger as de days go passin' by.
Dar ain' no means o' foolin' disshere 'sperience o' mine—
Dar's sumpin' gwine on inside dat watamillion rine!

Didn't show no moh pretentions
  Dan a squash some time ago;
Now, jes' look at dem dimensions!
  An' it still hab room to grow.
De stripes is showin' stronger; an' dat polish—ain't it
    slick?
It won't be many weeks until it's fitten foh to pick.
Each mo'nin' dat I notices I sees anuthuh sign
Dat dar's sumpin' gwine on inside dat watahmillion rine!

A NATURAL COWARD

Ol' Mistuh Trouble, he come aroun' one day
  An' say, "I gwinter get you, so you better run away!
I likes to see you hustle. Dats de way I has my fun.
  I knows I kin ketch up to you no matter how you run!"

I says, "Mistuh Trouble, you has been a-chasin' me
  Ever since I kin remember an' I's tired as I kin be.
So I's gwinter stop right yere an' turn aroun', a-facin' you
  An' lick you if I kin an' fin' out jes' what you kin do."

Ol' Mistuh Trouble, he looked mightily ashamed.
  He acted like a buckin' hoss dat's suddenly been tamed,
An' den he turned an' traveled off, a-hollerin', "Good day;
  I ain't got time to fool aroun' wif folks dat acts dat
    way."

LONG AGO

Long time ago—dat's yesterday—
De sun has traveled, so dey say,
Clean 'roun dis earth; de stars has shone,
An' den gone out; de hours has flown
Through sleep an' wakin' since de time
When dat ol' clock set out to chime
Upon de bell so sof' an' slow,
Dis very hour—a day ago.
We's had new work, since den, to do;
We's had new trouble to get through;
We's had new pleasures foh to make
Us overlok de ol' Time ache.
Ol' Time keep travelin' roun' de track;
Dar ain' no sense in turnin' back,
Upon de past, wif looks of woe,
'Cause yesterday—dat's long ago.

A HUSH-A-BY SONG

De leaves is a trem'lin' in de evenin' breeze;
    Hesh-a-by!
De starlight come a' siftin' th'oo de big pine trees,
    Don't you cry!
De hoot-owl holler an' de tree toad peep
An' de bull frog answer wif his voice so deep;
Dey ain' no proper company foh us to keep.
    Hesh-a-by!

De lightnin' bug is a-stahtin' for to roam,
    Hesh-a-by!
He's wusser dan de hoot-owl when it comes to goin' home.
    Don't you cry!
He nebber gits no honey 'cause de flowers is shet to stay,
Till Mistah Bee comes 'round a-callin' early in de day.
Dar ain' no sense in stayin' up an' actin' dat way.
    Hesh-a-by!

JUST AROUND THE CORNER

Dis life is like a road dat ev'ybody's got to travel.
Foh some it's rocks an' briars, an' foh others easy gravel.
  It's twistin' an' it's turnin',
  An' dar ain' no way of learnin'
What's waitin' roun' de corner. So jes' sing a little song;
Sing a little song an' keep journeyin' along.

Keep a trudgin', honey, even if it's stormy weather;
'Cause when you turns a corner, dat may change it
    altogether.
  If yoh footsteps grow uncertain
  An' de hardship gits to hurtin',
Jes' practice foh what's comin' an' do yoh bes' to smile;
Do yoh bes' to smile an' wait a little while.

THE LIGHTNING BUG

  De lightnin' bug, he started out
    A 'trabblin' froo de night;
  Says he, "De road is full of doubt,
    I wisht I had a light."

  An' so he flew up to de sky
    An' stole hisself a star;
  Says he, "Wif such a lantern,
    I kin journey near an' far."

  Dat shinin' star, it weighed so much
    It nearly made him fall
  An' any boy dat tried could clutch
    De lantern, bug and all.

  Sech doin's, honey, is what makes
    Some people lead a dance.
  De man dat steals his brightness takes
    A mighty sight o' chance.

A SUMMER DAY

In de mornin', when de sun was jest a-peekin' crost de
    edge
Of de cabin window ledge,
Like a little golden wedge
  A-pryin' loose de daytime fum de night,
I says, "Dis is de day I's g'ine ter do some work fo' sho'
An' I'll let de people know
What dey never knowed befo',
  Dat to slam aroun' an' toil is my delight.
I'll agitate de soil where corn is standin' in a row
An' git it interested in de way it ought to grow."

Oh, de mornin'-glories blossomed an' de birds was singin'
    gay—
If I plowed de groun' dat day
I might skeer 'em all away
  An' dat ain' no way foh any one to do!
An' purty soon de moonbeam come a-slidin' th'oo de tree
White an' shiny as could be,
Like a little silver key
  Foh to lock de daytime treasures far fum view,
Tomorrow, mebbe, I'll git up an' make another start.
My only botheration is, I's got a tender heart.

A WORD FROM THE ROADSIDE

  Never min' dat railroad,
    Never min' dat ship.
  Yoh uncle he des g'ineter walk
    When he go on a trip.

  Wheels kin keep a-buzzin'
    An' pass me on de street,
  But I keep movin' on my way.
    I's thankful foh my feet.

A VIRTUOSO

I sometimes has suspicions, in de toilin' an' de heat,
Dis life of ours is only a deception an' a cheat;
You's only hyuh a little while, an' often it do seem
Like all de sorrow's genuine an' all de joy's a dream.
But when de clouds is pilin' up at evenin' in the west
An' all de outdoor critters stahts de tunes dey likes de best,
De folks sits on de benches an' de chillun on de flo'
An' Eph'm takes de fiddle down an' rozums up de bow.

He never plays no book-learnt tune; de music dat he
    knows
Dar can't nobody study.   It's de kin' dat simply grows;
De kin' dat's trem'lin' in de trees, th'oo out de Summer
   hours
And sof'ly harmonizes wif de fragrance of de flowers.
Den Mistuh Trouble goes a slinkin' out.   He dasn' stay.
De lightnin' bug fotch lanterns so's he couldn' miss de
    way
Dat leads him off to No-wheres; an' dis life seems good
    foh sho'
When Eph'm takes de fiddle down an' rozums up de bow.

MAKING IT EASY

Tain' no use complainin'
   While you's travelin' along.
Keep yoh voice in trainin'
   Foh to sing a little song.

Tain' no use o' sighin'
   In a melancholy style.
You kin weep wifout half tryin';
   It's some credit when you smile.

LOOKING WEST

Over dar in twilight town,
When de sun goes driftin' down—
Driftin' to his place of rest,
'Mongst de shadows in de West—
Dat's whar things appear to me
Jes like what a town should be.
Castles risin' foh yoh view—
Shiftin', changin', always new.
Walls of crimson, seas of light,
Golden streets to lef' an' right.
Wouldn' I jes like to go
Dar, and not come back no mo'!
Dat's de place where all is gay—
While you look it dies away!
Dat's de way wif all yoh dreams,
Dat's de way wif all yoh schemes—
Glorious foh a litle while,
Den clean faded, like a smile,
Or a dew drop, or a rose,
Dat's de way de story goes.
Castles rise an' tumble down—
Same as dar in twilight town.

THE KNOWING BIRD

Ol'! Mistuh Blue Jay
    Yonder by de spring
Keeps on hollerin' ev'y day
    An' never says a thing.

Keeps on speechifyin'
    An' never feels no shame;
He knows a lot of human folks
    Is doin' 'bout de same.

SLIPPIN' BY

On a Sunday afternoon,
  Sittin' in de door,
Mammy Mandy sing a tune;
  Sing it o'er an' o'er;
"Feelin' most' indust'ous!
  Wish tomorrow'd come .
Ef 'twas only Monday
  I'd mek dat wash bo'd hum!"

Tuesday, Wednesday an' de lot
  Dey ain' none too long
Foh to fin' a restin' spot
  An' to sing a song.
Jes' six days a week she say
  Wis'ful-like an' glum:
"Ef 'twas only Monday
  I'd mek dat wash bo'd hum!"

Don't know what de trouble is
  Aftuh Sunday night,
Mammy get de rheumatiz
  An' ain't feelin' right,
But on Tuesday mornin',
  Feelin' better some;
Say, "Ef dis yere was Monday
  I'd mek dat wash bo'd hum!"

WISHFUL FISHING

Dis life wif happiness seems bright
  While you can hope an' wish
De mo' you never gits a bite,
  De mo' you wants to fish!

[75]

SUFFICIENCY

Oh, de snow it comes a-creepin'
  Froo de crack beneaf de do',
An' de win' it come a-sweepin'
  An' I shiver when it blow.
De drif's was gathered thick in
  De crotches o' de trees;
An' I had to eat de chickin.
  Ef I didn't, it would freeze.
Col' wave! Col' wave! Don't you come no mo'!
Don' you keep a-sighin' and a pryin' roun' de do.
I is livin' very patient. I is tryin' to behave,
But I doesn't want no mo'
     Col'
       Wave.

My vocal cawds is stretchin'
  An' dey hu'ts me when I sings;
An' de banjo, he is ketchin'
  Rheumatism in de strings.
An' de prices makes me holler.
  Dey sho'ly frets my soul—
A quarter of a dollar
  Foh a half a peck o' coal.
Col' wave! Col' wave! Don't you come no mo'!
Stop yoh pesterin' an' give de flowers a chance to grow.
I flounders in de roadway, an' I slips along de pave,
An' I doesn't want no mo'
     Col'
       Wave.

SMILES

'Tain' no use o' grievin', honey,
  When de skies is gray.
Cause a smile is always sunny
  Any kind o' day.

LITTLE JIM SCIENTIST

Dese explanation folks goes 'roun'
  A showin' off how much dey knows;
Dar nebber was a question foun'
  Dey couldin' answer, I suppose.
Foh Mistuh Wise I'll lay in wait
  An' when I meets 'im purty soon,
Dishere's whut I'll interrogate:
  "Who bus' dat corner off de moon?"

It come a-rollin' th'oo de sky
  So han'some an' so bright an' strong!
But as de Augus' days slipped by
  I notice dat dar's sumpin' wrong.
Dat ol' Nor'easteh blow an' whizz
  A singin' big, but out o' tune.
An' now de special question is:
  Who bus' dat corner off de moon?

He lef' de bay smashed up complete;
  He blew de sail mos' off de mast;
He broke de branches, slick an' neat,
  F'um trees dat fretted in de blast.
An' when sech damage kin occur
  In one short summer afternoon,
I has my s'picions who it were
  Dat bus' dat corner off de moon!

WHAT'S THE USE

De lazy man sits in de sun
  De bes' part of de day
An' brags of work he hasn' done
  An' kicks about de pay.

[77]

GIRL THAT BROKE MY HEART

Sometimes I pause and ponder in
   The midst of joy and strife
Upon the various women
   Who have influenced my life
And I harbor a suspicion
   That the girls who came between
Myself and hopes of happiness
   Are girls I've never seen.
There's one, a lady Samson,
   Who has spoiled my Heavenly hopes.
She turns my weekly laundry
   Into ribbons, fringe, and ropes.
I might contrive to don it,
   All festooned with dainty care,
If it weren't for the buttons
   That, alas, are never there!
When I am dressing for a party
   That's particularly neat
My drapery starts sliding toward
   My waist line or my feet.
In desperation forth I go
   And sit in pain and doubt,
As one by one the safety pins
   Turn slowly wrong side out.
I dream of her each night, I see
   Her fierce, relentless glare.
She takes a pair of pliers
   And she waves them in the air.
And every time a helpless
   Little button bumps the floor
She does another war dance
   With a wild, demoniac roar.
I know where I am headed
   For the things that I have said;
They're sure to queer the model life
   Which otherwise I've led.
When I've landed for my finish,
   In a place whose color scheme
Is superheated anthracite,

Backed up with smoke and steam,
I'll think, while for my sulphur bath,
I'm slid into the trough,
Of you, oh, heartless laundry girl
Who yanked my buttons off!

AN IDEALIST

Oh, tell not of dreams of the roses so sweet
When June scatters sunshine like gold at your feet;
Don't whisper the stories of lasting renown
To be won where the cannon all merciless frown.
If life's but a dream, as philosophers say,
Let me dream of a field where the home team at play
Awakens the skies to an echoing shout,
With three men on bases and nobody out!

Here's bliss undefiled as the crowd, running wild,
Invites to rejoicing man, woman and child;
Here's hope for the future, hope blossoming fast
And founded on glorious deeds of the past.
The thrill that goes surging throughout the great throng
Makes each pulse beat a measure both rapid and strong;
'Tis a moment that's fraught with magnificent doubt,
With three men on bases and nobody out!

Let the poet weave tales that are beauteous and strange;
Let the painter so skillful through wonderland range;
Let musicians create the soft mystical spell
That calls us 'mid sweetest illusions to dwell.
And yet, though the fancy of genius be fair,
There's nothing that it can bring forth to compare,
When you're looking for something worth dreaming about,
With three men on bases and nobody out!

STUMBLING BLOCK

A man once sat and pondered on the ways of this
    existence
  As he counted up a scanty store of pelf.
He sighed, "I've solved great problems as to housing and
    subsistence,
  But I somehow cannot do it for myself.
I can tell men how to labor while discouraging dissension,
And how to gain a fortune of superior dimension
While practicing philosophy to soothe the nervous tension;
  But I somehow cannot do it for myself.

"I can always solve a problem that relates to moral duty
  For each inquiring undecided elf.
I can show him how to lead a life of beatific beauty;
  But I somehow cannot do it for myself.
I can indicate just how the country ought to cut expenses,
And offer pleasant platitudes in all the moods and tenses
To show 'most anybody how he ought to mend his fences;
  But I somehow cannot do it for myself."

THE RIGHT TO LAUGH

"Some day," said I, "in idleness
  I'll be serenely gay;
Without a care to cause distress
  I'll laugh the hours away."

But when my holiday I'd try
  With pleasure to extend,
The task which once caused many a sigh
  Seemed a neglected friend.

The joy of which we hope to learn
  Dull indolence will spoil.
Even the right to laugh we earn
  Alone by simple toil.

AT THE BOOK COUNTER

Upon the counter where are shown the books
On which a nation with amazement looks,
Books that are fraught with scandal's morbid gloom
In desecration of each honored tomb,
There lay a volume which in bright array
Presented poems of a bygone day
And bade us pause all lovingly to note
The verses that James Whitcomb Riley wrote.

It was like blossoming that finds its way
To beauty in a region of decay;
A blossoming which is revived at last
And gently breathes the memories of the past.
It stilled the quarrel in the weary mind,
Reviving love for simple humankind
As in the turmoil it made bold to quote
The verses that James Whitcomb Riley wrote.

THE CLOCK

If you turn to work or turn to play,
  The clock keeps spinning along;
Your step may weaken from day to day,
  But its pace keeps brisk and strong.
Grinding, tirelessly grinding still,
It goes right on, like a mighty mill
Wrought by some cunning master's skill,
  Forever spinning along.
The years are ground into weeks and days,
  As the clock goes spinning along,
And the days into hours, as we lightly gaze
  And murmur a careless song.
And the hours that we fondly seek to stay
Are turned into moments so slight that they
Are tossed, at a breath, with our hopes away,
  As the clock goes spinning along.

SELF-ESTEEM

Although a thousand birds may sing
  A thousand strains of music sweet,
The crow will spread his sable wing
  And holler with a pride complete.
No matter what a man may hear
  Of eloquence from day to day,
He wants the neighbors to draw near
  And hark to what he has to say;
For nature, though her gifts be few,
  Lets every living thing rejoice
And lend ecstatic ear unto
  The sound of its especial voice.
And if a buzz saw could, somehow,
  Be made a vital, sentient thing,
Should some great tenor make a bow,
  'Twould say, "Shut up and let me sing."

MUCH LIKE THE PRESENT

My Uncle Jim dislikes the ways
Of all these young folks nowadays.
He says, with slow and stately pride,
"Their manners are undignified."
A friend who knew him in his youth
Has told us some amazing truth.
He showed some old daguerreotypes,
My uncle's vest had funny stripes.
His neckties would have made you stare.
So would his whiskers and his hair.
The current slang he talked with glee
And sang fool songs all off the key.
They say he even went so far
As practicing on a guitar.
And so, when now he strikes a pose
And sighs, "These times are not like those!"
The youngsters grin because, at last,
They know about his awful past!

THE OLD MUSIC BOX

Its tones were tinkling once and gay;
    But now, unheeded in the gloom,
It occupies, 'mid shadows gray,
    A dusty, unfrequented room.
Yet, carelessly I sometimes pause
    And turn the key and bid it sound
Despite the broken pegs and flaws
    Which so complainingly abound.

The melodies are old and queer—
    You scarce would think that years ago
They thrilled to every idle ear;
    And now for me alone they flow.
Even though cogs may squeak and jar
    And rhythms often feebly halt,
They call sweet memories from afar.
    I love the theme and pass the fault.

Perchance my lot or yours 'twill be
    Some time in shadows to remain
When we are worn and out of key
    And strive for harmonies in vain.
I hope some old-time loving friend
    Our dormant skill will deign to stir
And find us, even to the end,
    Not as we are, but as we were.

ELEMENTAL

Some little sentiment we've had
    That still is hovering near—
Perhaps a little song that Dad
    Would sing to Mother dear.
And though the calculations long
    Keep figures piling high,
Some things to every heart belong
    That money cannot buy.

AHEAD OF TIME

When good Columbus crossed the blue,
　Where dangers darkly hovered,
It's safe to say he never knew
　How much he had discovered.
He thought the beach of pearly sand
　And Injuns in the distance
Were all that gave this gracious land
　Its reason for existence.

He had no thought of buildings tall
　Or telephones or trolleys;
Of circuses or of base ball,
　Or fashion's fleeting follies.
Perhaps his shade across the Styx
　Remarks in accents surly;
"Fate loved to play me shabby tricks.
　I struck that place too early!"

NOT NEGOTIABLE

The poet sings his little lay
　Of silver linings in the cloud;
But that same silver wouldn't pay
　Your street car fare in any crowd.

The leaves that turn, the sun that sets
　Brings gold which other kinds outrank,
But what's the use of gold that gets
　No recognition at the bank?

The ripples on the gleaming wave
　He says are diamonds. 'Tis a joke.
For none of these, alas, will save
　The dreamer fond from going broke.

[84]

FUN WEARY

I'm wearying of the funny things
  That do not make me laugh,
For Time a trace of mildew brings
  That touches e'en the chaff.
I'm wearying of the pompous elf
  Who has grand tales to tell
And if he glorifies himself
  Believes that all is well.

I'm wearying of the fad and fake
  That makes the public shout
As from old hats magicians take
  The same old rabbits out.
Although a sense of humor clings
  As many things I see,
I'm wearying of the funny things
  That hold no laugh for me.

OLD ATHENIAN ARGUMENT

The women have a right to speak.
  We're reading still today
Of Lysistrata, not so meek,
  And wisdom's great display
By Moliere's ladies wise and fair,
  Whose fame can't be denied.
And so we venture to declare
  Xantippe had her side.

For, Socrates, whose words still please
  With classical renown,
Went out with Alcibiades
  By night to paint the town.
Xantippe stayed at home, severe
  In her housekeeping pride.
Philosophers are often queer.
  Xantippe had her side.

[85]

THE CHRISTMAS SAINT

There must be moments, good old saint,
    When all the sorrow you behold
Will leave your smile exceeding faint
    That beamed so confident of old.

There must be moments, as in vain
    You seek repose so nobly won,
When your warm heart cannot refrain
    From grieving o'er the tasks undone.

There must be courage in good cheer,
    And often with a saddened heart
You whisper, "Gentle friends draw near
    And say with me, 'I do my part!'"

THE DODGER

Talk about your autos and the way they burn the air—
The speed that they are making doesn't really compare
With the swiftness that's expected from the average
    citizen
Who gets into the hustle and the bustle, now and then.
He's got to keep on dodging to the left or to the right,
He longs to teach his muscles the rapidity of light.
If you feel yourself unwilling to be cut down like a flower,
You've got to side-step at the rate of sixty miles an hour.

Dodging airplanes as they whirl in strange delirious glee;
Dodging grafters all alert wherever you may be;
Dodging consequences when some foolish thing is said;
Dodging some dictator who decides to punch your head;
No wonder men get nervous as the days go rushing by.
The Nation's indigestion isn't wholly due to pie.
This life's a constant study to develop speed and power
When you must side-step at the rate of sixty miles an hour.

WORTH THE WAITING

It ain't no use complainin',
   As has been remarked before,
When you never get a nibble
   As you fish along the shore.
You should always keep your temper
   Though the disappointments come,
But this life's a whole lot sweeter
   When the fish
       bite
          some.

You should always smile a little
   Though the luck don't come your way;
But you'd like your turn at gettin'
   An excuse for laughin' gay.
It's "never mind the weather"
   When the outlook's keepin' glum.
But it's "glory hallelujah!"
   When the fish
       bite
          some.

RATES

It won't be so long ere the song of the sea,
And the sunshine that glistens so bright and so free,
   Will tempt us to wander once more
Where the Summer hotels are so thick and so tall
That the view you can buy is exceedingly small
   Of the waves as they break on the shore.

But each year we assemble and faithfully try
To obtain all the pleasure our purses will buy;
   And we figure by day and by night
On a debt whose small items will hourly increase,
Where freckles are twenty-five dollars apiece
   And mosquitoes cost ten cents a bite.

ST. PATRICK'S DAY

St. Patrick's day!   St. Patrick's day!
　And here you are again
To drive all evil things away
　From hillside and from glen!
'Tis like a gentleman you try
　To banish from the scene
All ugliness as spring comes by
　A-wearing of the green!

The violet with timid charm
　Is waiting to draw nigh,
But winds that fill her with alarm
　Come muttering from the sky.
So never mind the toads or snakes
　But let your might expand
To chase away the cloud that makes
　The trouble in our land!

AN OLD FRIEND

I wouldn't mind the waking
　When the engine starts a row;
The noise it once was making
　Would be music to me now.
And I fain would see the cattle
　Racing down the track again,
All stampeded by the rattle
　Of the Old * * * Freight * * * Train!

I wouldn't mind the shrieking
　Of the whistle any more;
I wouldn't mind the creaking
　And the grinding and the roar.
My mood is very humble
　As I lift the sad refrain.
I long to hear the rumble
　Of the Old * * * Freight * * * Train!

LONG DISTANCE

We've listened to all that you told us
  Of colder an' warmer an' fair,
An' sometimes we've thought that you'd sold us
  Fur fun, but we didn't much care.
It's easy, with nerve and persistence,
  To tell what we'll get purty soon,
But it's time to turn on the long distance:
  Say, what do you know about June?

Who cares for your talk of tomorrow?
  The springtime is fickle we know,
But there's weather that banishes sorrow,
  Beyond, past the chill and the blow.
When each creature that warbles or chatters
  Seems to join in the general tune,
Cut out these plain day-by-day matters.
  Say, what do you know about June?

BOY AND MAN

Gazing into the window
  And wishing with all his heart,
The small boy stands on the busy street
  That has turned to a Christmas mart.
It seems so fragile, that pane of glass
  That shuts in the lights and toys!
He gazes into the window,
  A stranger to all its joys.

Gazing into the future,
  The man with the wistful eyes
Sees visions of pleasure or content,
  Or many a splendid prize.
And the curtains of chance that screen them
  Are slight, yet so hard to part;
He gazes into the future
  And wishes with all his heart!

HITCH HIKERS

Santa Claus avenue, up neath the star
That shines, ever faithful, to guide us afar.
I stand on the curb and my thumb I extend
And say, "Won't you give me a hitch hike, old friend?

"Won't you let me go riding with you for a while
On the journey that passes the tear or the smile
Which memory holds since the years long ago.
Like landmarks still clear in the sunshine or snow?

"Will you give me a ride to the place that I knew
When I played hide and seek by the chimney with you?
The highway's your own, so resplendent and wide.
I'm asking, old friend, will you give me a ride?"

THE PEDESTRIAN

He looked about with air distraught,
    And cried in tones of woe;
"I'm wondering which way I ought
    In quest of peace to go.
The streets are filled with motor cars
    Which pass me madly by;
There will be airplanes 'mid the stars
    If I should learn to fly.

"E'en in the ocean depths profound
    Strange craft I'd dodge in vain
And should I burrow 'neath the ground
    I'll meet a subway train.
Unto a state of nervous stress
    My life is surely linked,
My only chance for happiness
    Is to become extinct!"

PHRASEOLOGY TO THE RESCUE

Ol' Bill Jinkins started in a-seein' things at night;
He also caused a scandal by a reg'lar family fight.
We all said Bill was drinkin' rather oftener than he should
An' 'lowed he warn't any credit to the neighborhood.

He wouldn't change his program, though his friends all
      talked their best,
An' finally a warrant was got out fur Bill's arrest.
An' jes' 'bout then an uncle died 'way out near Kankakee
An' left ol' Bill as rich as any one could wish to be!

So Bill, he hired some lawyers—I dunno how much he
      spent—
An' proved that he was sufferin' from artistic
      temperament.
An' as fur seein' things—Bill's on a very lofty perch—
They say that he's engaged in psychological research.

Now everybody looks at him with interest and awe.
It ain't fur us to criticise opinions of the law.
An' yet we can't help speculatin' on where Bill would be
If 'tweren't fur that uncle somewhere's out in Kankakee.

ON THE LADDER

To useful methods let us stick,
    Nor pause to quarrel as we climb;
It is worth while to lay a brick,
    To throw one is a waste of time.

OVER AND UNDER

We ask the financier with dread
To tell about his overhead,
And in some profits we demand
That he explain his underhand.

"I'm going to live in the country," said the city man one day.
"I'm going to revel in the song of birds and the perfume of new mown hay.
I'm going to gather the blossoms bright and gaze on the butterfly,
And list to the mythical melodies when tremulous branches sigh."
But the bird he heard was the querulous owl which kept him awake at night.
The insect he met was a hornet; and his was a sorry plight.
In the course of his botanizing he gathered a poison vine,
And he hurried away to the station and said, "It's the city, boys, for mine!"

"I guess I'll go up to town awhile," said Uncle Bill one day.
"I'll have a look at the 'lectric lights an' be careless an' downright gay!"
He looked in vain for thoughtless glee in the crowds that went madly by;
He got mixed up with a motor car and a cabman hollered "Hi!"
He ate a dinner he didn't like, and went to a dreary show,
And slept in a room just six feet square and he murmured "I guess I know
When I've had enough. At break of day I'll be headed for home, you see.
The city's the place for city folks, an' the farm is the place for me!"

A FLEETING GLIMPSE

He talked incessantly of art,
But most admired the graceful skill
With which engravers can impart
True meaning to a dollar bill.

KINDLY ASSURANCE

Have you wandered through the mountains?
    Have you watched the gurgling rill?
Have you listened to the fountains
    As they tumbled down the hill?
Have you felt the perspiration
    'Neath your collar form a pool?
Have you heard the exclamation—
    "But the nights are always cool!"

Where the ocean sands were broiling
    Have you walked with weary feet,
While the mercury was spoiling
    As it stood out in the heat?
Have you heard the haughty menial
    Perched upon an office stool
Say in accents mildly genial,
    "But the nights are always cool!"

Some day I may be going—
    Though I hope I shall escape—
Where the brimstone lake is flowing;
    And I'll see some dreadful shape
Grinning as he turns me neatly
    With a pitchfork as a tool.
And I bet he'll warble sweetly,
    "But the nights are always cool!"

STRAWS

A straw vote on a New Year's eve
May show results that will deceive,
Because the straw was somehow found
Too much inclined to twist around
Or limply sink into a state
Which made it hard to calculate.
That straw, it somehow came to pass,
Was saturated in a glass.

JACK AND MOLLIE

'Tis a dear old-fashioned place,
    And the roses love it;
Blossoms spilled with lavish grace
    Round it and above it,
Yearly weave a fairy spell
    O'er the spot so charming,
Up where Jack and Mollie dwell,
    Making love and farming.

Near-by runs the road to town;
    Trouble takes it straightway;
Never thinks of turning down
    Toward their leafy gateway.
Joys from elsewhere made to roam
    By dull melancholy
Stop and make themselves at home
    There with Jack and Mollie.

Mollie stops her work to laugh,
    Jack stops his to listen;
Sunbeams are not bright by half
    As her eyes that glisten.
If a fond thought whispers low,
    Loving lips will drop it;
They are old enough to know
    Better than to stop it.

It is sweet when life seems cold
    And the world is lonely,
Such a picture to behold,
    Though in day dreams only.
Laughing at the care that kills,
    Safe from folly's harming,
Jack and Mollie mid the hills
    Making love and farming.

THE ELFIN FROGS

There's a group of busy builders over yonder by the lake,
  They are building up the Maytime and the June.
They work till late at night. At early morn they are
      awake;
  As they toil they have their own especial tune.
It is cheering to the neighbors thus to hear them at their
      labors,
  While they give each bough another coat of green.
They're artistically building when the sunshine brings
      new gilding,
  As the frogs direct another Summer scene.

They are building up the willows for new shadows in
      the pool,
  Where the grasses will so gracefully incline.
They are planning for the roses, by their own especial rule,
  Which has always brought so beauteous a design.
Some think that they are joking and will soon be merely
      croaking,
  But we wise ones know exactly what they say.
They are builders, still aspiring with a purpose all untiring
  To create another perfect Summer day.

NO CLOSED SEASON

We can protect the game that roams
  Where huntsmen go in ardent quest;
We can protect the humble homes
  Where wild fowl pause to feed or nest.

Humans uplift a cry of pain
  While mighty volumes fill the shelves
And ask somebody to explain
  Why we cannot protect ourselves.

MELODY

'Tis wonderful music when summer draws nigh
And the south wind is sweet with a laugh and a sigh,
The blossom's temptation entices the bee,
The robin is happy up there in the tree;
'Way down in the valley and up on the hill,
The world is a-tune with the hum and the trill,
And the clouds in the sky that go sailing along
Seem to loiter and wish they might join in the song.

And there's ne'er a philosopher living could find
A word in it all that appealed to his mind;
And there's ne'er a musician on earth who could fail
To see that it breaks all the rules of the scale.
And yet there was never a melody made
By the songster whose lay is a trick and a trade
That is one-half so sweet as the laugh and the sigh
And the hum and the trill as the summer draws nigh.

LONGING

I care not for the halls where art
   Is spread before the eye;
I care not for the mummers smart,
   With mimic laugh or sigh.
I care not for the statesman's speech,
   Nor for the poet's scrawl;
I want to hear the bleachers screech
   When some one says, "Play ball!"

The sacrifice a statesman makes—
   To be most frank and blunt—
In me small interest awakes.
   I want to see a bunt.
The fearless motorist and bold
   Sets not for me the pace.
I'm simply yearning to behold
   A slide to second base!

THE ILL-NATURED MAN

When you see a feller scowlin' an' a-lookin' mighty glum,
  Like he wants to take this world an' wring its neck;
When he gives a surly answer, like he wished a crash 'd
      come,
  An' leave the solar system in a wreck;
When he don't take any notice of the children in their
      play
  But trudges on resentful an' alone,
Don't hold it up against him that he isn't blythe an' gay,
  'Cause maybe he has troubles of his own.

There's folks that acts peculiar when there's sorrow in
      their hearts,
An' you ought to find excuses more or less
If they shut their teeth together when some old remem-
      brance starts
  An' makes 'em envy others' happiness.
We can't all be philosophers an' bear our burdens well
  When thorns remain, an' all the flowers have flown.
Don't shut him from your sympathy in loneliness to dwell.
  'Cause maybe he has troubles of his own.

CAUTIOUS

Though airplanes gaily ride on high,
I shall not journey through the sky;
It is too far to take a chance
On getting to an ambulance.

EYES OF AFFECTION

We wonder why, when children show,
  As fathers tell, such mighty wit,
They always as they older grow,
  Get so completely over it.

[97]

A PLEA

Say of my friend the worst you may.
   Say that in folly's paradise
He lived a hapless gilded day,
   Uninfluenced by good advice.
Say that like some o'er-weening king
   He squandered where he should have spent well.
But say not that contemptuous thing,
   "He meant well!"

Call him a rogue, if you should think
   That he deserves so harsh a name,
But do not bid him cringe and shrink,
   Some empty pitying phrase to claim.
Spare him, since now misfortune rules,
   A fate where all, not long since, went well
That stock apology for fools:
   "He meant well!"

A VAIN DESIRE

We dream of idle hours whose song
In murmuring measures drifts along.

The bee that toils in fierce unrest,
The bird that tends its cherished nest,
The cloud on high that sails the sky
Fulfill a duty ere they die.
The tiniest insect in its flight
Is fain to do some task aright.
The petals of the fading rose
Show beauteous change, but not repose.

We vainly seek in mortal pride
What to all else has been denied.
'Tis whispered, 'mongst the very flowers,
"There are, in truth, no idle hours."

[98]

THE SLEEP SONG

Over the river the breezes come stealing.
  The willows nod drowsily there.
The days of the Summer have oft been revealing
  Long hours of tempestuous care.
Where the afternoon sun loitered on with his smiling
  The shadows all silently creep,
And the breeze softly murmurs in tender beguiling,
  Singing the old world to sleep.

A blossom nearby, from a twig lightly shaken,
  'Midst the fallen leaves rustles and gleams;
It brings a caress that would soothe but not waken
  A weary one drifting to dreams.
The spell of the Winter will soon be displaying
  A loneliness silent and deep,
From the realms of the twilight the breezes come
    straying
  And singing the old world to sleep.

UNINFORMED

I don't pretend to know for sure
  What "relativity" may be,
But lack of knowledge I endure
  In matters closer far to me.
I do not know what calls the smile
  Into a little baby's face,
Nor why a war's relentless guile
  Should horrify the human race.
I do not know why men defy
  The precepts they themselves unfold,
And are bereft of honor by
  The mystic influence of gold.
And so, philosopher, I pray
  Do not disprove my wit so slow,
Since I encounter every day
  So many things I do not know.

THE OLD CLOCK

My uncle Jim, he has a clock.
    He bought it years ago.
It used to sound a smart "tick tock,"
    But now it's kept for show.
It used to move with nimble hands
    To count the minutes o'er,
But now its record always stands
    At strictly half-past four.

"It's weary now," said Uncle Jim.
    "It did its work right well;
And fading into memories dim
    Are tales it used to tell.
It sort of halted on the way
    It went so well of yore.
And, finally, it stopped one day
    Right there, at half-past four.

"That is the hour when I awoke
    To greet the dawn anew,
And next the hour that softly spoke
    Of toiling almost through.
My old clock tells of early days
    And of the rest in store;
And so I simply let it stay
    Content at half-past four."

COMPENSATION

Nay, do not despair, though the rose has a thorn,
    And disdain all its blossoming fair.
Nor turn from life's pleasures with doubting and scorn
    Because of regrets hidden there.

The smart is forgotten and past in a day
    'Mid the joy that the flowers disclose.
Too oft must we suffer with naught to repay.
    It is well when the thorn has a rose.

EARLY RECOLLECTION

Tousle-haired, freckle-faced, ordinary boy,
Went to school with him, you know.
  'Twas his greatest joy
To be dodging lessons—very much like all the rest.
Fished and went in swimming, and was very simply
     dressed.

Everybody knows him well. Wears a high silk hat.
Makes profound addresses now and then on this and that;
Has a manner most sedate, and is, to tell the truth,
The pride of the community—a model for our youth.

But as I look upon his face with well-remembering eyes,
I still discern a likeness which the years cannot disguise;
And still he seems, howe'er his time he chooses to employ,
That tousle-headed, freckle-faced, ordinary boy.

THE DRAWBACK

I haven't any railway stocks to irritate my mind
  When interstate embarrassments arise.
In the movements of the markets it is not my fate to find
  A thing to agitate me or surprise.
I haven't any interests in the corporations great,
  Nor dealings with the crafty lawyer folk.
Nobody ere reviles me as a danger to the state.
  I'd be happy—if I only wasn't broke.

There's no one camping on my trail with philanthropic
    plans
  For which I am supposed to have the cash.
I never risk my fortune to annex another man's,
  I'm quite immune from speculations rash,
I have no motor car to keep me worried night and day.
  This life would seem a long and gentle joke,
Except for one slight hindrance that is sadly in the way.
  I'd be happy—if I only wasn't broke.

CARL A. RUDISILL
LIBRARY
LENOIR RHYNE COLLEGE

THE AUTOMOBILE

It's fine when the world is an automobile
    That merrily whirls you along,
Where the sunshine is bright and the stars seem to feel
    In humor for laughter and song.
It's fine when the motor with steady refrain
    Keeps up its reliable pace,
And there's never a reason to fret or complain—
    But it's fierce when a breakdown takes place.

A mile is a trifle. The flight is so swift
    That we scarcely know how it was made,
Nor think of the chance to give some one a lift
    Who is toiling on foot up the grade.
It's fine when the world like a motor car glides,
    With nothing its progress to balk,
But it's fierce when it skids or it stalls or collides,
    And you find you must get out and walk.

So, let's bear in mind, when it's our turn to speed
    At a rate that is swift and secure,
The fellow compelled on his way to proceed
    At a gait that is plodding but sure.
Then stifle your pride as you thoughtlessly plan
    A scare with the whistle or gong,
And remember to leave right of way for the man
    Who has to keep trudging along.

WEARINESS

Sometimes you grow weary of weeping
    And wish for a smile or a sneer
To banish some thought that is creeping
    Close by in the shadows of fear.

There's relief in a moment of chaffing
    Of things you may hear or may read.
But when you grow weary of laughing
    Your plight becomes sorry indeed.

A STAR-LIT NIGHT

A star-lit night.   A whispering fragrance starts
   From yonder clover field.   The fireflies gleam;
The singers of the night with bursting hearts
   Pour forth their melodies.   'Tis like a dream
Of something longed for in the dreary hours
   When all the world was chilled by Winter's blast;
A dream of peace afar amid the flowers
   Where sorrow sleeps; a dream come true at last.

Such kind repose must surely be unknown
   To those whom Envy bids us hold in awe.
Not to the tyrant trembling on his throne.
   Nor to the man whose gains defy the law
Can such slight things appeal—and yet far less
   Their fierce and fond endeavors must requite
Than the sweet spell which banishes distress,
   The benediction of a star-lit night.

THE HOURS

So slow they go!   So slow!   So slow!
The hours of waiting and of woe!
When we must toil till set of sun—
It is so long ere day is done.
The hours of darkness feebly grope
Toward morning, when, untouched by hope,
The pendulum swings to and fro.
So slow they go!   So slow!   So slow!

So swift they shift!   So swift!   So swift!
The hours when pleasures gayly drift
Adown the sun-kissed stream of time,
With silken sails of love and rhyme.
These are the truest and the best,
Worth all the rigors of the test,
But vanished like an elfin gift,
So swift they shift!   So swift!   So swift!

[103]

RAINBOWVILLE

Started out one Summer day
For Rainbowville, not far away.
Fine location, we were told,
Where you just picked up your gold;
Never saying, "If you please";
Always living at your ease.
Just beyond the maple hill
Fortune smiled, in Rainbowville.

Past the fields, where ripening grain
Glistened with the recent rain;
Following still the prismed light
Till it faded from our sight;
Where the willow bough inclines,
Where the honeysuckle twines;
Through the orchard, past the mill,
We kept on toward Rainbowville.

Weary, footsore, cold and wet,
Hunger, mingling with regret,
Bade us turn to childish rest—
Next day we'd renew the quest,
And we did. Ambition fond
Ever lures to the beyond.
Years have passed, and we are still
On our way to Rainbowville.

THE PROMISE

Full well I know that somewhere dwell
    The violet and the blushing rose,
Though vanished from the field and dell,
    Now bleak and touched by many snows.

And vanished joys, full well I know,
    That make the present day seem vain,
Like blossoms hid beneath the snow,
    May, in time's passing, smile again.

DREAMS AND DEEDS

The dreamer turns from the tumult dire,
  And dwells in a world apart;
Yet he ever mourns with the vain desire
  Of a weary and empty heart.
But his lamentations abruptly stop
  When the wintry breezes blow,
And he finds there is wood he will have to chop,
  And it's time to be shoveling snow.

And it's good to be caught in the tingling blast
  That says: "You shall strive or fall!"
To awaken from dreams of a futile past
  And the joys we can ne'er recall.
The blood grows redder through every drop,
  With the quick, reviving glow,
When we face the wood that we've got to chop,
  Or get ready to shovel snow.

'Tis better to dare the tempest's roar
  And the storm's unyielding stress
Than fan the ember and bar the door
  And sigh for forgetfulness.
So send the blaze to the chimney top,
  And toil that the path may show
Which you fain would tread. There is wood to chop,
  And it's time to be shoveling snow.

INFINITESIMAL EGO

The world is a wealth of delightful impressions.
  Today we are here and tomorrow we're gone.
We give and we take. The demands and concessions
  Are strange, but we smile as the story goes on.

The struggles for pelf are but minor digressions.
  A sunset today and tomorrow a dawn
Are things in themselves prompting humble confessions.
  The Fates play the game, and a man's but a pawn.

[105]

TO THE WORLD

Oh, gentle world, whose smiling skies
Are bluer than the bluest eyes,
Whose whispering as the wind draws near
Is sweetest music to mine ear,
Pray listen while this mood is lent
To wooing and to compliment.
To thee my fondest hopes incline,
To thee I pen my Valentine.

Full well I know what grief they find
On whom you turn a gaze unkind.
They dwell apart from joy and light,
Chill is their day and dark their night.
And so men press, a hurrying throng,
With thought and toil, with jest or song,
Each hoping his reward will be,
Oh, gentle world, a smile from thee.

ART AND NATURE

Airplane hurrying past a cloud
Seems a creature strong and proud.
It reflects the sunset sky
Like a giant butterfly.
Swiftly, in majestic flight,
It will fade away from sight,
Secrets of the air to learn—
Sometimes, never to return.

Waiting, as the months go by,
For the real butterfly
Where the sunbeams, day by day,
'Mongst the perfumed blossoms stray.
Better than yon work of art,
With an engine for a heart,
Seems this being, I confess,
Born of Nature's loveliness.

THE HAIRCUT

I used to kick about the way
   That mother cut my hair.
She made it look like new mown hay
   All scattered here and there.
I used to seek some distant nook
   Far from the girls and sob,
Because that haircut made me look
   Like a dejected squab.
But now my wife goes out with me
   To buy my hats and shoes.
The salesmen chuckle when they see
   The things that she will choose.
The shoes are of the sportive plan.
   High-silken is the lid.
One end of me is clergyman,
   The other college kid.
My neckties when we go to call,
   All in our best arrayed,
Will cause the paper on the wall
   To pine away and fade.
It fills my soul with dumb regret,
   When I my wardrobe scan
And think of all the laughs I'd get
   Were I some other man.
My strange reflection I discern
   With mutinous surprise.
To boyhood I would fain return
   And then apologize.
What though the neighbors laughed aloud
   And father dear might swear!
I would be grateful now, and proud,
   If mother cut my hair!

THE SHIP

We are looking for the rainbow that is hid behind the
    storm.
When this hurricane is ended we will help the world
    reform.
Youth smiles with shining eyes and wisdom has a
    furrowed brow;
The ship sails on—but everybody wants to show it how.

One calls for heroism in a hard remorseless fray,
Another seeks philosophy with intellectual sway
While prayers ascend in reverence to consecrate a vow.
Earth must improve, since everybody wants to show it
    how.

When fervent motives clash with purpose confident and
    high
We know that calm must yet reveal the rainbow in the
    sky.
We know the ship of state will ride with jewel-glistening
    prow
And we know we have men at the helm to guide and
    show it how.

VOX POPULI

The banquet puts upon display
    The Imp of the Perverse,
And makes folks offer talk which they
    Neglected to rehearse.

With interest they're always heard
    As fancy they engage,
But hunger always speaks the word
    That's read on history's page.

A CHEERFUL GIVER

I haven't made a fortune yet,
    An' mebbe never will;
In lots o' things I've failed to get
    The needful luck or skill;
I've somehow always missed my guess,
    Exceptin' once or twice
In small affairs; but none the less,
    I like to give advice.

I've had hard knocks enough, you see,
    To teach me lots o' sense.
I won't be stingy, no, sirree,
    With my experience.
I've been a loser at each game,
    From Wall street down to dice,
An' elsewhere, too. But jes' the same
    I like to give advice.

It's something which, you must admit,
    A lot of people need,
Although it doesn't always fit,
    It can't be guaranteed.
There ain't no laurels on my brow
    Fame's plaudits to entice.
I've made mistakes, but, anyhow,
    I like to give advice.

PUBLICITY

The politician strikes a pose.
    We pause to have a look.
Along with beauties in the shows
    He has his picture took.
Just what he wears we may discern
    And what he eats and drinks,
Yet all in vain we seek to learn
    Precisely what he thinks.

[109]

BOND OF SYMPATHY

He said he loved the mocking bird,
  With lay so boldly sung.
He spoke not of the strife that stirred
  Where reckless speech was flung.

He mentioned not opinions grave
  Upon some sporting chance,
Nor thoughts of those who spend or save
  In realms of high finance.

He may be brave to do and dare
  In the ambitious throng,
And yet his heart has time to bear
  The burden of a song.

And so in deep content I heard
  His greeting kind extend.
He said he loved the mocking bird.
  I knew he was a friend.

ON BETTER ACQUAINTANCE

Of course the blossom had to fade.
  The parting brings a sigh.
And next to us will be displayed
  The snowflake from the sky.

And if we will but pause to scan
  This visitor so fine
We will admire its fragile plan
  Of texture and of line!

Much which at first with dread we knew
  Has shown a kindlier pow'r
And been on more familiar view
  As lovely as a flow'r.

REFLECTION

Within a sylvan pool there springs
A stagnate world of swarming things.
Grotesque and strange they throng and press
Complete in their unloveliness.

Above it nests a creature gay
With light poised wings in quivering sway.
It gazes down, but only sees
The bright sky mirroring through the trees.

The bird sings on in joy complete
'Mid blossoms delicately sweet—
Our world, like this small scene, we know
Has many shapes of grievous woe—

And yet it need not seem unkind,
Since to the contemplative mind
It must reflect in guise sincere
A higher, nobler atmosphere.

ACHIEVEMENT

If in your heart you have one note of song
    To which the world as yet has never thrilled,
And you can give it to the listening throng,
    Life is not vain.   A mission is fulfilled.

If you can plant the blossoming of a smile
    Secure where weeds of care were wont to grow,
Or lift the weary burden for a while,
    For some poor pilgrim overborne with woe.

The gentle thoughts which, at your name shall rise,
    Are better, truer praise than that which falls
To him whose palaces have pierced the skies,
    While flattery runs to greet him as he calls.

THE LONELY ROAD

Along the lonely road I sped.
My lights shone dim, not far ahead.
And shadows strange cast by the moon
Threw hints of danger threatening soon.
There, near a hilltop or a bend,
The lonely road appeared to end.
Yet threatening shadows melted there
Before the headlights' faithful glare.
When the ascent or turn was made,
The road unwinded through the glade
Until, at last, the journey done,
The warmth of home and hearth was won.
Through weary hours and days and years
We journey on, 'mid shadowy fears
And think strange barriers bar the way
To human reason's flickering ray.
Still we go on.   The road unwinds
And each his destined object finds
And smiles as he reviews at last,
In warmth and cheer, the shadowy past.
So, let's be on, since men must roam!
The loneliest road still leads to home.

THE SETTING SUN

Old Father Time, the avaricious elf,
Adds golden days to his uncounted pelf,
And hides them, in his ruthless love of gain
Where wistful memories plead and seek in vain.

Amid a cloak of clouds, the glowing sun
Fades from the view.   The twilight has begun.
Old Father Time, still eager to purloin,
Into his purse has dropped another coin.

GREAT INVENTION

A man with a curious glint in his eye
  Exclaimed, "With dismay I am filled
By hearing wise people so frequently cry,
  'Behold how the beans have been spilled.'
An inventor am I with a wonderful gift
  And by patient endeavor I mean
The gathering gloom that surrounds us to lift.
  I'll invent the non-spillable bean.

"We've been told in the song how our best plans go wrong
  Through a blunder that none could foresee;
And when we were going so swift and so strong
  A careless word shattered our glee.
They'll hold me the greatest inventor of all
  When the world I have made quite serene.
For such a result any toil will seem small.
  I'll invent the non-spillable bean."

THE OBSTINATE CINCINNATUS

He jes' didn't want to be bothered, he said,
When they mentioned the life that he quietly led.
They told him they thought he could certainly claim
A measure or so on the trumpet of Fame.
But he told 'em the songs of the birds and the bees,
An' the wind as it swept through the wakening trees,
An' the whisperin' wave as it broke on the shore
Was music enough, an' he wouldn't ask more.

He said that to hear 'em yell "Zebedee Jones!"
E'en with patriot fervor inspirin' their tones,
Would break up the harmony nature reveals
If you let it alone. Vain are all the appeals
To hustle him forward to join in the fray.
He's busy, he says, in his own little way
With a life that seems fair, though its scope is but small.
An' he jes' doesn't want to be bothered; that's all!

PENANCE

When the sky is hung with mist
  An' it starts to rain,
Then your feelin's get a twist
  That you can't explain.
All the sadnesses of the years
  Come in dark array,
Driftin' with the tide of tears
  On a rainy day.

How we bruised the laughin' flowers
  'Neath our careless tread!
How we wasted golden hours
  Scoffin' as they sped
At the simple joys they brought
  Far from pomp an' fray!
Things seem different when we're caught
  By a rainy day.

All the smilin' an' the song
  From existence flee;
All the world is goin' wrong—
  Leastways seems to be.
Then you struggle to repent
  Of your errin' way.
Can't be much worse punishment
  Than a rainy day.

THE SUN

When shadows fall across the heart
  The sun shines on and will not show
A willingness to hold a part
  In sorrow that we mortals know.

His duty has been well surveyed;
  For selfish grief it finds no room,
For human tears could not persuade
  A single violet to bloom.

PERILS OF TALK

Oh, bitter yet insidious fate
So oft the finish of the great!
What melancholy mishaps grow
From some few sentences which show
A heart too generously inclined
To educate the public mind!
A flow of speech all gratis stirred
That waits not for so much per word
Promotes a state of feeling sad.
Oh, how is glory to be had?
One man attains a lofty lot
By frequent eloquence, red hot.
Another wins Fame's kind caress
Because of silent pensiveness—
Which seems, indeed, the safer plan,
Since all the history of man
No sadder tale than this can tell:
"He talked not wisely, but too well!"

THE FLIGHT

"Come fly with me!" the young man said,
    "Not in the crude old-fashioned way.
My aeroplane soars overhead
    And frets the bonds that bid it stay.
'Tis but a pleasure jaunt I ask
    You'll try with me.
This is no life-long journey's task—
    Come! Fly with me!

"The fervid phrase of other days
    Has given way to simple fact;
No more poetic fancy plays—
    Our speech is simple and exact.
I don't request you'll live life through
    And die with me;
I merely am inviting you
    To fly with me."

ENDLESS TASK

Oh, Lazy Day! Oh, Lazy Day,
   Where have you been so long?
We thought to loiter on the way
   And pause for Summer song;
We thought to serenade the sun
   That dozed into the west
In gratitude for having won
   Another day of rest.

However idle hands may be,
   The hour that slowly goes
From leaden care cannot be free
   That banishes repose.
The chain of thought forged link by link,
   By days of hope or fear,
Holds us. We are compelled to think—
   And that's a task severe.

PATIENCE

It takes a heap o' week days
   To prepare for Sunday's rest;
It takes a heap o' ripenin'
   Till the fruit is at its best;
It takes a heap o' practice
   Till you learn to sing a song—
A lot o' patience is required
   To push this world along.

It takes a heap o' weather,
   Goin' every kind o' way,
Before we see the splendor
   Of a truly perfect day.
An' it often takes long sorrow
   Ere you earn the right to smile,
But it sure is worth the waitin'
   To be happy for a while.

JABEZ

Oh, Jabez Jones, he never does a thing to make things
    right.
He simply views the world's events from morning until
    night,
And even when the stars above, like distant lanterns burn,
He'll sometimes catch a comet that's performin' out of
    turn.
He isn't much at plowin'. He is clumsy with a hoe.
He lets the other people plant the crops an' make 'em
    grow.
He isn't even cheerful, with a story or a song.
His one accomplishment is tellin' folks when they are
    wrong.

He'll meet you when your hopes are risin' confident an'
    great
An' tell you why you're jes' too soon, or why you're jes'
    too late;
He'll take your calculations an' he'll speedily explain
Jes' how you'll miss the answer you were sure that you'd
    attain.
Oh, Jabez, we will miss you when it comes your turn
    to go.
The man who writes your epitaph will hesitate, I know,
In tryin' to express your praise in language smooth an'
    strong
For fear you'll rise right up an' say he's gettin' it all
    wrong!

OLD METAL

The merry pedler now proceeds to hurry through the land
Inquiring, "Friend, what have you to be sold at second
    hand?
Some values have been rising while some other values sunk.
Have you some scraps of gold that you might care to sell
    for junk?"

THE MINUTE

The clock ticked out a minute light
   Upon a Summer day.
I said, "The moment is so bright,
   Why won't you stop and play?"
It answered, "Twould disgrace me quite.
   I must be on my way—"

"For I must turn, as I take flight,
   New buds to blossoms gay,
And help the cool and restful night
   To supersede the day.
Although my work seems only slight,
   I must be on my way.

"I lead youth toward ambitions bright,
   I touch man's hair with gray—
An atom to make up the might
   By which Time holds his sway—
We small things keep the great aright—
   I must be on my way."

LAUGHTER

Here's to the laugh that seems to tell
Of a state of mind where all is well;
The laugh that ripples with humor gay,
Like a flash of sun on a gloomy day!

But who shall echo the laugh that shows
A friend's mistake or a foeman's woes,
The laugh that is empty and insincere,
The laugh that only conceals a sneer.

DEFIANT

A man once started out to set
   This world upon its feet.
He viewed its follies with regret
   And sympathy complete.
Its difficulties to allay
   He burned the midnight oil
And wrote or lectured, day by day,
   With unremitting toil.

His hair hung long and likewise thin,
   His whiskers grew awry;
His clothes grew shiny 'neath his chin;
   He didn't wear a tie.
And then he heard the old world say,
   "Each to his own design.
Enjoy yourself, my friend, your way,
   And I'll keep on in mine."

WHEN SNOW FALLS

Goin' to sleep? I don't blame you, Old Earth,
   As you call for a cover of snow.
It's no use to weep and there's no call for mirth
   As the wearisome hours come and go.

The blossoms have fled. It is time now to rest
   While the storm clouds relentlessly creep.
Though much that we dread is, of course for the best,
   I don't blame you for going to sleep.

[119]

SEPTEMBER

Now and then a leaf
　　Comes drifting down,
Its verdance all too brief
　　Turned to sullen brown.

Now and then a bird
　　That sang so gay
To flight aloft is stirred
　　And goes his way.

Now and then a flower
　　Fearing the frost
In an autumnal hour
　　Fades and is lost.

Now and then a friend
　　Faithful and fast
At his journey's end
　　Leaves us at last.

MOCKING BIRD

When Spring draws near, the mocking bird
　　Defies the wintry roar.
A sunbeam speedily makes heard
　　The song we loved of yore.

Though sullen be the sky above
　　And fierce the icy blast,
We know we'll find that song we love
　　In triumph heard at last.

Tempestuous might must bring dismay—
　　The slight must fear the strong—
Yet storm can never find a way
　　To still the heartfelt song.

[120]

THE MOUNTAIN DWELLER

I ask no odds of the men who ride
  With trappings that gleam like gold;
Nor envy the homes where they abide,
  Nor the lands by their will controlled.
For a sense of freedom and joy profound
  Is mine as I look on high.
There's only an acre or so of ground,
  But billions of acres of sky.

'Tis a heartless master, the stubborn sod,
  As for beauty you delve and strive;
You must blast the quarry and break the clod
  Ere gardens and towers may thrive,
But my clouds with castles each night are crowned
  And the radiant stars draw nigh—
There's only an acre or so of ground,
  But billions of acres of sky.

Oh, the town is great and the town is fine,
  And it's gay as a town can be,
And the house on the height where the sun's ashine
  Is humble, though fair to me;
But a universe seems to gather round,
  With joys that will never fly;
There's only an acre or so of ground,
  But billions of acres of sky.

CONFIDENCE

It is not to the friend we strive to show
Our courage and our strength, but to the foe,
Or to the stranger, passing on his way,
Who seeks to overwhelm with proud display.
But, as in childhood, when the day was through,
In loving faith we turned to those we knew.
Only to those we love may we confess
The night's foreboding and the weariness.

ALWAYS HANGIN' 'ROUND

When the air is growing chill and the sky, across the hill,
　No longer shows the coloring so proud,
There will shine a lingering ray of a bygone Summer
　　day—
　　There's a sunbeam always hangin' 'round the cloud.

There's a hope for every fear; there's a rainbow in each
　　tear
　And a braver thought in every head that's bowed
By the passing weight of grief.　There is a promise of
　relief.
　　There's a sunbeam always hangin' 'round the cloud.

Even to the stormy blast there must be an end at last,
　If the proper time and patience are allowed.
There's a promise ever true in a silvery bit of blue.
　　There's a sunbeam always hangin' 'round the cloud.

FIERCE UNREALITIES

There are troubles that leave us to sigh with relief
　And be glad that at last they are through.
They are better by far than the permanent grief
　Of the trouble that never comes true.

There's rest for the weary in toil or in fight
　When a genuine ill comes to view;
But there's dire apprehension by day and by night
　Of the trouble that never comes true.

In humanity's struggle I'll welcome my share,
　Only asking, as hope smiles anew,
That my heart may be free from the shadowy care
　Of the trouble that never comes true.

[122]

TWILIGHT TIME

A perfumed sigh from the meadow bloom
Floats out on the night; through the woodland gloom
Comes the lonely note of the whippoorwill,
Singing with scant but honest skill,
   A fare-thee-well to the day that's gone,
   And a hope for the day that's yet to dawn.

The sky is pierced by a million stars;
In the fields the shadows smooth out the scars
That the plowman made; and the insect crowd
Raises a chorus shrill and loud,
   A fare-thee-well to the day that's gone,
   And a hope for the day that's yet to dawn.

Ah, this is the hour of the day that's best—
The hour that is neither toil nor rest,
When the task we have struggled with departs
And the thought of the future revives our hearts
   With a fare-thee-well to the day that's gone,
   And a hope for the day that's yet to dawn.

A PICTURE

A line of hills and a billowing mist,
A splash of waves on the pebbled shore,
Where the roots of the great trees gnarl and twist,
As a light wind flutters the surface o'er.

A lake that has found a place so high
That it can mirror without delay
Each passing mood of its comrade sky
In loyal sympathy, day by day.

How vain is the painter's splendid skill
To hold enchained by his arts so strange
The beauty that shifts and is never still,
And grows more wondrous with every change.

[123]

THE LILACS

The sun hotly blazed on the long, dusty street
   That leads to the hurrying mart,
And the wearisome spell of the languorous heat
   Seemed to penetrate e'en to the heart.
And yet, like a memory, distant and dim,
   There came through the foliage dense
A perfume—it banished the frowning so grim—
   Of lilacs from over the fence.

The wayfarer paused, and there came to his mind
   The old-fashioned place of his birth;
Illumed by a face that was gentle and kind,
   The gentlest and kindest on earth;
The big, rambling garden, the nook where a boy
   Dreamed of a future immense;
Where the sunbeams would linger in laziest joy,
   And the lilacs hung over the fence.

Again to the journey, again to the strife,
   And yet, 'mid the toil of the day,
A faint, subtle odor, with memories rife,
   Full oft through the air seemed to stray.
The smile had a meaning which no one could learn,
   That lightened his features so tense,
As the perfume, in fancy, would sweetly return
   Of lilacs from over the fence.

HOUSE CLEANING

When celebrations great are gone
   Next day we start anew.
We have to face the cold gray dawn,
   With further work to do.
Through clouds the sun will shine on high,
   Effacing care and doubt.
We'll sweep the cobwebs from the sky
   And shake the rainbows out.

ALWAYS

'Tis the sunshiny song and the laughter
  That give life its greatest alloy.
No sorrow that darkens thereafter
  Can blot out an hour of true joy.
Though the season be bitter and cheerless,
  We know what the waiting is worth,
And we face it contented and fearless
  Till June treads the blossoming earth.

When winter is stern and depressing,
  A sky momentarily blue,
Or a breeze from the south, half caressing,
  Brings radiant visions to view.
In fancy the rose that has vanished
  Blooms forth, while a bird carols clear.
The storm and the stress soon are banished,
  But summer survives the whole year.

THE ROAD ALONE

From far away through the wood so still
Comes the sobbing note of the whippoorwill;
The moon that rises so cold and white
Stares at the world with a look of fright,
And the trees in the shadow toss and moan
When you're trudging the weary way alone!

Another time, what a friendly note
Has the whippoorwill with the tireless throat!
The moon has a jolly face and round,
As jolly a face as could be found,
And the sigh of the wood is a tranquil song
If someone with you is trudging along.

ONCE IN A WHILE

Once in a while, like the sun that streams
  Through the breaking clouds on a day of showers,
The light of happiness gaily gleams
  On this wistful, wearysome world of ours.
And the sands of the hour-glass turn to gold,
And melodies faint and far unfold,
And they lightly clink and our thoughts beguile
With mystical music—once in a while.

Once in a while, through the battling crowd,
  The face of an honest friend will pass
Or a voice will silence the tumult loud—
  The tender voice of a loving lass.
But the throng grows fierce and the din grows high
As hope and hatred renew the cry,
And a frown effaces the careless smile
That comes to cheer us—once in a while.

Once in a while comes the day that's "best,"
  After days of waiting through "worse" and "bad."
The day that is radiant and sweet with rest,
  The day that we long for when life is sad.
How well 'twould be if the tide of years
Could be, somehow, turned from the flood of tears;
If the hours of darkness and doubt were drained
And only the "Once-in-a-while's" remained!

FADED JOKES

The mother-in-law life now reveals
  As a protecting saint.
When slipping on banana peels
  The laugh becomes more faint.
Old jokes no longer can amuse
  As in the days gone by,
And mostly when we read the news
  We simply want to cry.

THE ENDED DAY

Good night.
  The firefly's tiny spark is gleaming,
Now faint, now bright.
  The moon across the rippled wave is beaming
  With golden light.
A summer day with all its blossoming glory
Is done; yet like some old and favorite story
  'Twill fondly linger, even in our dreaming—
Good night.

Good night.
  The woodland zephyr softly playing
Across the height;
  The honeysuckle's perfume gently straying
  In languid flight,
Fall on the weary sense with touch endearing,
Like whisperings far too faint for conscious hearing,
  As if the world, at last grown kind, were saying,
Good night.

WINTER SONG

Outside the window sings a bird.
  Inside the room an empty cage
Hangs where his singing would be heard,
  Our tenderest kindness to engage.

And yet he scorns the proffered ease
  And waits beneath the sky so drear,
Lifting a lay himself to please,
  And confident that Spring draws near.

He waits to meet what time shall bring,
  Reliant on himself alone,
And says, "I only ask to sing
  Of life and freedom, all my own."

[127]

CASTLES IN THE AIR

There's a building boom in No-Where-Land—
It's one that comes each year,
When the spring is new,
When the skies grow blue,
And the south wind whispers cheer.
With fancy as architect, we've planned
(His charges are small but fair)
Improvements great
For each vast estate,
And our castles in the air.

It's only a minute we need to see
The minarets and towers
In beauty rise
'Neath our very eyes,
And these treasures are all ours.
Your likes may be fickle and strange and free
For easily you repair
The wreck that falls
When the old charm palls
In your castles in the air.

When the golden rivers of twilight start
And the scarlet sun sinks low,
It's a journey slight
To that land of light
Where the maybe blossoms grow.
And it's only the friend with the honest heart,
Who has followed through ill and fair,
Who can be your guest
As you dream and rest
In your castles in the air.

THE HORIZON

"Just out yonder," the youth declares,
   "I have seen where the earth and the heavens meet.
'Tis a long slight line, and the one who dares
   May cross it with confidence complete.
And some day I'll build me a swift-winged boat
   And I'll speed to the land of the golden glow,
Where the twilight landscapes shine and float
   And comfort the dreamer here below."

" 'Tis not far distant," the man cries out,
   "The time when peace shall maintain its sway
In this world that struggles 'mid storm and doubt—
   The journey is such a little way!
We will swiftly speed on the wings of thought
   To the glories opened before our view!"
And the man forgot as he smiled and wrought
   The hope of his youth that had ne'er come true.

UNENDING

The wind is telling a story
   As it sweeps o'er hill and vale,
And the moon in her distant glory
   Smiles at the quaint old tale;
A tale of the morn's bright gleaming,
   A tale of the noon so clear,
A story of daytime dreaming
   And of night with its shadows drear.

The stars are carelessly smiling,
   And the rippling water's flow
Laughs at the wind beguiling
   With this tale of long ago.
And the days and the nights succeeding
   Ravel and weave and blend,
While the world laughs on unheeding
   The story that has no end!

VIVAT MEMORIA

*The following poem written for the occasion was de-
livered by Charles B. Hanford at the conclusion of the me-
morial services in honor of Major Archibald W. Butt, held
at the National Theatre in Washington, May 5, 1912:*

Life—the mysterious gift
From the Eternal Source—
How variously do we find it used
Ere it is claimed again,
We know not why or how!
We squander or we let it idly rust;
We lend our days, in petty usury,
In hope to add another's little share
Of earthly happiness unto our own,
And still the solemn shadows lurk beyond
And bid us falter in our futile quest.
In weariness we pause and lift our eyes
And wait for someone, wiser than the rest
To show the way and teach us to defy
The Darkness and the Shadows—Over There!

Then from the Many Thousands, one steps forth!
No stern, compelling soul, but kind of speech
And generous of thought;
A man who loved this world of ours so well
He felt no fear of what it might contain
And had a smile, even for death itself.

He showed the way.
And as he passed he found
The comradeship of natures like his own,
First among men because they were content
To be the last.

There was no stress of storm where he went down,
No vengeful hate nor strife of jealous greed.
Oh splendid Rivalry!
Where loyal men stood forth in lofty calm
And like the Master of our Christian faith

Unhesitating, gave their lives to show
The others how to live.

Now, as we say "farewell," we strive to speak
The words which lingered often in our hearts
Words of affection and admiring faith.
How tenderly we bring earth's sweetest flowers
To one who sees them not with mortal eyes;
So men 'mongst their gentlest thoughts withhold
Until they serve alone
To soothe the selfish sadness of the living.

Farewell, dear friend.   We recognize you now—
One of the favored few to whom God gives
A mission to perform.
We bid farewell unto the least of you,
Your mortal self.
The real man you were—the man you are—
Will live among us always.

The bugle will sound "taps".   Our tears will fall
Into the vastness of the silent sea.
The reverent Hymn will rise
A requiem sweet in which the World must join
And yet the Love that gives us men like you
Will never let the parting be complete;
For in this life where souls like shadows pass
The only great and true Realities
Are such as Memory tenderly enfolds
In changeless Love and Honor
Ever more.

SOME DAY

Some day, some day 'twill all come right,
   The tangled skeins will all unwind
And we will grasp the colors bright
   And leave the somber threads behind.
The sun is low and rest is sweet,
   Yet fears draw round us when it sets;
And sorrow comes with winged feet
   And joy but heralds new regrets.

E'en while we taste, sweet draughts will turn
   To bitterness that hurts us sore;
We learn to love and, loving, learn
   To feel the loved one's loss the more.
And yet, when "reason's" light grows pale,
   There shines through darkness still a ray
Of faith untaught which can not fail,
   And leads us onward to some day.

THE END OF THE ROAD

There's always an end of the road, you know,
Though the journey seems long and rough and slow.
In the country shade or the thriving town
Your journey will end if you don't lay down.
It may seem weary and bleak and chill
As you toil to the top of the misty hill,
And see from its summit no rest in store,
But a way that looks rougher than before.
You may flinch from the smart of the stinging pain,
As you set your face to the sleety rain,
And think with a fierce, resentful sigh
Of a blossoming path and a star-strewn sky.
But sooner or later, a glow so warm
Will shine from a window through the storm,
As Happiness beckons your footstep slow—
There's always an end of the road you know.

"30"

(The Symbol of the day's work well performed)

Let us be mindful of the friends so dear
Who have departed.
Not only in the silence of grief
But in the companionships they loved to share
Let us remember those who go before.
Their work is done.   The life of each stands forth
Fair as the printed page on which he wrought.
From day to day their deeds and thoughts they placed
In a relationship correct and sure
To show more plainly than the types could tell
Their messages of Hope and Helpfulness
To those they loved.
By their example we who linger here
May work with truer skill as we compile
The vast, mysterious universal book
To which all men must give, who pass this way.
Their Much, their Little—but their all in all.
And may we be like these, when we in turn
Complete the Task
And hear the Voice of Conscience gently say:
"Your labor well performed
Has made you worthy of The Great Reward."
The form is closed—the proofs are verified
And all is well
Good night
And Sweet Repose!

"DAWNWOOD"